Successful Writing

INTERMEDIATE

Virginia Evans

Express Publishing

Published by Express Publishing in 2000

Liberty House, New Greenham Park, Newbury, Berkshire RG19 6HW
Tel: (0044) 1635 817 363 — Fax: (0044) 1635 817 463
e-mail: inquiries@expresspublishing.co.uk.
INTERNET http: //www.expresspublishing.co.uk.

© Virginia Evans, 2000

Design & Illustration © Express Publishing, 2000

Colour Illustrations: Nathan

ISBN   1-903128-50-1

Acknowledgements

Author's Acknowledgements

We would like to thank all the staff at Express Publishing who have contributed their skills to producing this book. Thanks are due in particular to: Sean Todd (Editor in Chief), Andrew Wright (senior editor), Anna Miller (editorial assistant), Mary Stevenson (senior production controller), the Express design team, Tony Boyle (recording producer) and Erica Thompson, Anne Whitman, Steven Gibbs and Sally Pierce for their support and patience. We would also like to thank those institutions and teachers who piloted the manuscript, and whose comments and feedback influenced positively the production of the book.

Photograph Acknowledgements

© **Reuters** for photographs on p. 48
© **Audio Visual** for photographs on pages: 78, 81, 107

While every effort has been made to trace all the copyright holders, if any have been inadvertently overlooked the publishers will be pleased to make the necessary arrangements at the first opportunity.

ABDULLAH

abdhbey2009@yohoo.com.

Contents

UNIT 1 Part A Guidelines for Writing

TYPES OF COMPOSITION

When you write a composition you need to understand the type of writing required. Your piece of writing can be in the form of a **letter**, an **article** for a magazine/newspaper or a **report**.

LETTERS are written to a person (e.g. your pen friend, a newspaper editor, etc) or a group of people (e.g. the students' society, the local football club, etc) for a specific reason (e.g. *to give advice, to make a complaint* etc). They include:

- **Informal letters** to people you know well, written in a personal chatty style.
- **Formal letters** to managers/officials etc, written in a polite formal style.
- **Semi-formal letters** to people you do not know well or people you know but you want to sound polite and respectful e.g. a teacher of yours, your pen friend's parents, etc, written in a polite and respectful style.

ARTICLES are found in magazines and newspapers. The following can be found in the form of an article:

- **Descriptions** of people, places, buildings, objects, festivals, ceremonies etc.
- **Narratives** about real or imaginary events which happened in the past. They can be written in the **first person** (first-person narratives) when the writer is the main character of the story or in the **third person** (third-person narratives) when the writer is describing events which happened to another person or group of people.
- **News reports** about current/recent events (e.g. fires, accidents, etc) written in impersonal style. News reports present facts objectively and unemotionally.
- **Reviews** discussing a film, TV programme, book, restaurant, etc and recommending it or not to the reader.
- **Discursive essays** about arguments concerning particular subjects. They include:
- **"For and Against" essays** which present the pros and cons on a specific topic
- **Opinion Essays** which present the writer's personal opinion on a specific topic
- **Providing Solutions to Problems** which discuss a problem and its causes, making suggestions and mentioning the expected results and consequences
- **Letters to the Editor** which present the writer's personal opinion on a specific topic or the writer's suggestions on a specific problem.

REPORTS are formal pieces of writing and have a specific format and features. They include:

- **Assessment reports** discussing the suitability of a person, place, plan, etc for a particular purpose, job, etc.
- **Proposals reports** discussing suggestions or decisions about future actions.

1 Read the extracts (A-G) and decide which type of writing they are from (1-7).

1	third person narrative		5	informal letter
2	formal letter		6	description of a person
3	first person narrative		7	description of a festival
4	description of a place			

B As the last band played their final song, I felt sad that the festival was about to end. All the fun moments of the week passed through my mind in a split second. Dancing to the beat of the music, I looked at my friend and said, "I can't wait until next year's Jazz Festival!"

C Dear Aunt Carol,
I'm sorry about not replying to your letter sooner but I've been extremely busy.
Guess what! I finally found a position as a nursery school teacher in Brighton! Isn't that wonderful?

D Debbie is tall, slim and attractive, with long brown hair and beautiful blue eyes. She likes wearing smart clothes and always looks good.

A Dear Sir/Madam,
I am writing to complain about the service I received during a visit to your restaurant on 8th November.
Firstly, I had booked a table for eight o'clock, but when we arrived, our table was not ready and it was half an hour before we were seated. I was very annoyed.

E When I opened my eyes, bright sunlight was streaming through my bedroom window. As I was about to get out of bed, I heard a noise coming from the kitchen downstairs.

F Aruba is a tiny island in the Caribbean Sea. It is only 29 kilometres off the north coast of Venezuela. With its white sandy beaches and clear blue waters, Aruba is the perfect place for a relaxing holiday.

G It was a bright, sunny morning when Jill Wilson waved goodbye to her mother. "Have a nice day at school — and be careful!" called Mrs Wilson. The birds were singing as Jill stopped on the old wooden bridge to look down at the ducks on the water below.

2 Read the extracts (A-G) and decide which type of writing (1-7) they are from.

1	proposal report	5	assessment report

2	for and against essay	6	news report

3	review	7	opinion essay

4	essay providing solutions to problems

A Four people were killed and eleven were seriously injured when two planes collided on the runway at Leland Airport early this morning.

B All in all, I believe that newspapers play an important role in our lives. They keep us informed about world news as well as providing interesting reading material.

C To begin with, one of the main advantages of studying abroad is that you have the chance to learn another language. Moreover, you experience a different culture and way of life.

D
To: Ms M Timms, Personnel Manager
From: Mr T Brown, Senior Assistant
Subject: Assessment of Robert Dunkan
Date: 15th February, 20...

Introduction
The purpose of this report is to assess the suitability of Robert Dunkan for the position of Sales Manager for our shop in Brunwick.

E *Firstly, all blocks of flats should be provided with large rubbish bins. In addition to this, residents should be allowed to throw out their rubbish only at night. This would result in reducing the amount of rubbish in the streets during the day.*

F The cast is excellent and Michael J. Fox is perfect as the voice of Stuart Little. With the use of computer animation, Stuart looks more like a real mouse than a cartoon mouse, convincing viewers that he is a miniature actor.
The combination of computer animation and live action is superb.

G **Recommendation**

I believe that the course of action proposed above will attract more customers to the White Dove Restaurant. Not only will the Italian seafood and vegetarian dishes draw more people to the restaurant, but the live music will also greatly improve the restaurant's atmosphere.

UNDERSTANDING RUBRICS

To plan your composition you need to understand the rubric i.e. the composition instructions. Read the rubric carefully and underline the **key words/phrases** which will help you decide what you will write about. Key words/phrases indicate:

- the **imaginary situation** you will write about (e.g. *You are a reporter .. to write about a fire which broke out last night ...*) This can also suggest who you are (e.g. a reporter), what has happened (e.g. fire broke out), etc.
- the **imaginary reader** who is going to read your piece of writing (e.g. *the manager of the company you work for has asked you to write ...*). This will help you decide on the **writing style** i.e. the appropriate style of language - formal/informal, etc you should use.
- the **type of writing** (e.g. *a letter, an article describing an event you attended,* etc)
- the **specific topics** you should include in your answer (e.g. *describe the place and comment on its good and bad points*)

Study the example below.

¹You work for a travel magazine. Your ²editor has asked you to ³write an article discussing ⁴the pros and cons of air travel, including factors such as cost and convenience.

1	situation
2	reader
3	type of writing
4	specific topics

3 Read the rubric below and match the numbers to the following headings:

- *reader* ....
- *situation* ......
- *specific topics* ....
- *type of writing* ....

¹Your ²best friend is spending the summer in your country and needs advice. Write a ³letter ⁴advising him where to go and what to do and telling him approximately how much money he should bring.

4 Read the rubric and circle the correct answers to the questions that follow.

You work in a local tourist office. The manager has asked you to write a report on a new restaurant which has just opened in your town. Write your **report** describing the restaurant, the food and the service there and commenting on its good and bad points.

1 Who is going to read your piece of writing?

2 What is the situation?

3 What type of composition should you write?

4 What specific topics should you include?

5 a) Read the rubric and underline the key words, then answer the questions.

You are a writer for an international English-language magazine. Your editor has asked you for a short article about a famous person from the twentieth century that you admire. Write your **article** about the person, describing his/her personality as well as the reasons you admire him/her.

1 What type of composition is this?
   A a third person narrative
   B a formal letter
   C a descriptive article
   D a review

2 Who is going to read your composition?
   A your best friend
   B your editor

3 Which of the following statements are true? Circle.

A You should write about a famous person you have met.

B You must describe his/her personality.

C You should give reasons why you admire this person.

D Your article should be about a famous artist or scientist of the eighteenth century.

E You may include your own feelings about the person.

4 Which of the following topics *must* you include? Circle.

A The advantages and disadvantages of being famous.

B Personal qualities and characteristics.

C Information about the person's family background.

D Reasons why you admire him/her.

b) **Which of the two people below would *not* be suitable for your article? Why?**

Johann Strauss
1825 - 1899

Mother Teresa
1910 - 1997

BRAINSTORMING FOR IDEAS

- Write down any ideas, words and phrases that you can think of which relate to the specific topics of your composition.
- Group your ideas, crossing out any irrelevant ones, and put them into a logical order.
- Check that your ideas are relevant to the topic(s) in the rubric.

6 **a)** **Read the rubric in Ex. 5a) again and tick the topics that you should include in your article.**

- why you admire the person ....
- looks and appearance ....
- personality ....
- hobbies and interests ....

b) **Look at the words/phrases below and say which topic from above they are linked to.**

- helped those in need
- selfless
- compassionate
- courageous
- entire life was devoted to others
- donated money to charity
- patient

PLANNING THE LAYOUT OF YOUR COMPOSITION

Your ideas should be organised into paragraphs. The layout of most types of writing consists of three parts: an **introduction**, a **main body** and a **conclusion**.

I **Introduction**

The introduction, i.e. the first paragraph, is a short paragraph whose purpose is to give the reader a general idea of the subject of the composition. It should attract the reader's attention so that he/she wants to continue reading.

II **Main Body**

The main body usually consists of two or more paragraphs and its purpose is to develop points related to the subject of the composition. The number of paragraphs and the way you divide them depends on the specific topics of the composition. Each paragraph should deal with points related to the same topic. Whenever you discuss a new topic, you should begin a new paragraph. For example, in a for and against essay the main body should have two paragraphs: one discussing the points for, and another discussing the points against.

III **Conclusion**

The conclusion is a short final paragraph in which you can summarise the main idea of the subject, restate your opinion in different words, make general comments, express your feelings, etc.

7 **a)** **Which of these topics should you include in the *introductory paragraph* of an article describing a person you admire? Circle.**

A final comments about the person

B who the person is and why you admire them

C what the person looks like and what type of clothes they like wearing

7

b) Which of these topics should you include in the *conclusion* of your article?

A general comments and feelings about the person
B personal qualities of the person
C background information and achievements of the person

8 Read the article and label the paragraphs with the headings below. Then answer questions 1-3.

- *final comments/feelings*
- *personal qualities*
- *reasons you admire her*
- *person's name and reason you chose her*

Introduction

The person I admire most from the twentieth century is Mother Teresa. I regard her as one of the kindest and most caring people the world has ever known.

Para 1
....
....
....

Main Body

Mother Teresa was a selfless person. She devoted all of her time to others and never put her own needs first. She was also very courageous and never thought about the risks she was taking when looking after people who were sick or dying.

Para 2
....
....
....

What I admire most about Mother Teresa are her achievements. Her entire life was devoted to charity work. For example, in 1952 she opened a centre in Calcutta for the terminally ill, where patients could be cared for and die with dignity. She also won many awards, including the Nobel Peace Prize in 1979. She donated the money from her awards to fund other centres. Even though Mother Teresa is no longer with us, these centres still operate, offering help to those in need.

Para 3
....
....
....

Conclusion

I admire Mother Teresa not only because she was a generous and kind-hearted person, but also because her accomplishments have influenced people all over the world. It is hardly surprising that since her death in 1997 she has been regarded as a true saint.

Para 4
....
....
....

1 Who is the article about?
2 What justifications are given to support the statement that "Mother Teresa was a selfless person"?

3 Which of Mother Teresa's achievements are mentioned? What examples are given?

TOPIC SENTENCES & SUPPORTING SENTENCES

- Main body paragraphs should begin with topic sentences. A **topic sentence** introduces or summarises the main topic of the paragraph and gives the reader an idea of what the paragraph will be about.

- The topic sentence should be followed by **supporting sentences** which provide examples, details, reasons, justifications and/or evidence to support the topic sentence.

topic sentence ➤ **There are many disadvantages to air travel.**

supporting sentences ➤ Firstly, plane fares are extremely high. For example, if you choose to travel from London to Manchester by train, you will definitely pay less than you would if you travelled by plane. Moreover, being on a plane for hours can be tiring.

9 Read the article in Ex. 8 again, underline the topic sentences in the main body paragraphs and then replace them with the ones below.

1 There are good reasons why I admire Mother Teresa so much.

2 Mother Teresa was a truly self-sacrificing person.

10 a) **Match the topic sentences to the paragraphs. There is one extra topic sentence that you do not need to use.**

1   For one thing, there are far too many cars on the roads.
2   There are many arguments in favour of banning cars from city centres.
3   However, a city centre without traffic does have its disadvantages.

  A ....
In the first place, it would help to reduce pollution. This means that the city centre would be a healthier place to live and work in. Furthermore, it would be easier for pedestrians to walk around the centre without having to cross busy roads.

B ....
For one thing, shop owners would lose business as customers might find it inconvenient to travel to the city centre by public transport. Moreover, for those who live in the city centre, life would become quite difficult as they would not be able to park their cars near their homes.

b) • Which part of the composition do these paragraphs belong to — the introduction, the main body or the conclusion?

• What do you think the topic of this composition is?

• What type of composition are the extracts from?

11 **Read the topic sentence in bold, then choose the most suitable supporting sentences (A - D) to complete the paragraph.**

On the other hand, there are arguments in favour of tourism. ....
....
....
....
....

A   Firstly, tourism can help reduce unemployment in an area because of the jobs it provides for local people.

B   Furthermore, tourism can spoil the natural beauty of an area.

C   What is more, the profits from tourism can be used to improve roads, hospitals and schools.

D   In addition, restaurants and souvenir shops overcharge customers.

12 **Read the topic sentences below and think of appropriate supporting sentences to complete each paragraph, as in the example.**

e.g.   Catherine is a very pretty teenager. *She is tall and slim with dark skin and long curly hair. She usually wears jeans and T-shirts.*

1   My father is a handsome man.
   ....
   ....
   ....
   ....

2   Nicole is a very sociable person.
   ....
   ....
   ....
   ....

13 **Read the paragraphs below and think of appropriate topic sentences to complete them.**

A ....
....
First of all, it is cheaper than buying designer clothes which can be very expensive. What is more, if you make your own clothes, you can design them exactly the way you want them.

B ....
....
To begin with, medical research can be very expensive. Moreover, such research can take years to show successful results. Last but not least, lots of time is often wasted on experiments which do not work.

9

LINKING WORDS AND PHRASES

- Linking words/phrases make your writing more interesting to the reader, and easier to understand.
- Some linking words (e.g. *and, because, but, so, since*, etc) can join two short sentences into one longer sentence.
  e.g. *He is clever. He is hard-working.* ➡
  He's clever **and** *hard-working.*
  Ann is happy. She passed her exams. ➡
  Ann is happy **because** *she passed her exams.*
- Some linking words/phrases (e.g. *In addition, What is more, However, On the other hand,* etc) show how ideas are related either between two sentences or two paragraphs.
  e.g. *I have written to you three times already.* ➡
  I still have not received a reply from you.
  I have written to you three times already. **However,** *I still have not received a reply from you.*

first complaint { Firstly the employees who delivered the cooker were extremely rude and careless. While installing the appliance they made a considerable mess, then they left without tidying the kitchen up.

adding more points

second complaint { **Furthermore,** after they had gone, I noticed that the cooker was badly scratched and the operating instructions were missing. ...

Linking words/phrases can be used to:

- **show time:** when, whenever, before, while, as soon as, etc
- **list points or show sequence:** first(ly), to start with, next, finally, etc
- **add more points:** furthermore, moreover, in addition, and, also, what is more, etc
- **show cause or effect:** because, since, as a result, so, consequently, etc
- **give examples:** for instance, for example, such as, especially, etc
- **show contrast:** however, on the other hand, despite, though, etc
- **introduce a conclusion:** all in all, to conclude, to sum up, finally, etc
  (for more examples see Appendix I)

14 Circle the correct linking words/phrases, as in the example.

1 Mobile phones are expensive (**but**)/**so** they are very convenient.
2 She is very generous and shares everything. **Since/On the other hand**, she can be moody at times.
3 Growing your own vegetables is cheaper than buying them. **Even though/What is more**, home-grown vegetables are usually tastier.
4 Many young people are taught computer skills at school. **Despite/As a result**, they have a better chance of finding a job.
5 I admire Jackie **because/therefore** she has found happiness in both her professional and private life.
6 Air travel is the most expensive form of transport. **All in all/However**, it is the fastest.

15 Read the extract and fill in the correct linking words from the list below.

for example, what is more, as a result, on the other hand

Watching films at the cinema has many advantages. To begin with, modern cinemas are usually equipped with the latest technology. 1) .... , films have better picture and sound quality. 2) .... , you can see all the latest films as soon as they are released.

3) .... , going to the cinema has certain drawbacks. 4) .... , the price of a ticket can be expensive and cinemas are often crowded, especially at weekends.

16 Choose the correct linking word/ phrase to join the sentences.

1 Simon failed the exam. He had not studied enough. (**since, while**) ....
....
....

2 Ordering take-away food is very convenient. It can be rather expensive. (**although, such as**) ....
....
....

3 Aaron wanted to go to the football match. His mother wouldn't let him. (**but, therefore**) ....
....
....

4 Adventure holidays can be very tiring. They can be quite dangerous. (**but, and**) ....

5 It started getting cold. I put on a jumper. (**so, as**) ....

6 The hairdresser said it was perfectly safe. The chemicals in the dye made my hair turn green. (**even though, also**) ....

17 Replace the linking words/phrases in bold with synonymous ones from the list below.

despite, as, even though, such as, therefore

1 **While** I was walking home I saw an accident.
2 He was born in Poland **so** he can't be Spanish.
3 Your mechanic took three days to fix my car, **in spite of** the fact that it required only minor repairs.
4 There are many places to visit in Rome **like** the Colosseum, the Trevi Fountain, and the Pantheon.
5 **Although** Rachel is allergic to dogs, she loves them.

WRITING TECHNIQUES

There are a variety of writing techniques you can use to make your composition more interesting to the reader.

To begin or end your essay you can:

— **address the reader directly** i.e. write as if you were speaking to him/her.
e.g. *You can imagine what life would be like without water.*

— **use direct speech** to give somebody's exact words, **a quotation** from a famous person or someone who has influenced your life, **a proverb** or **a saying** (i.e. a well-known phrase). In all cases it is necessary to use quotation marks.
e.g. *After all, "An apple a day keeps the doctor away."*

— **use a rhetorical question** i.e. a question that does not expect a reply.
e.g. *What would modern society be like without computers?*

● **You can start a narrative by setting the scene** i.e. by using the senses to describe the weather, atmosphere, surroundings and also to create mystery and suspense.
e.g. *It was a cold winter's night. The wind was blowing hard as Jack was walking down the dark empty street.*

● You can also use **a variety of adjectives, adverbs and verbs** to make your composition more attractive to the reader.
e.g. *"Hold on!" Helen screamed to Bob as she desperately tried to help him get out of the freezing water.*

18 Read the following beginnings and endings and identify which writing technique(s) the writer has used in each.

1 Why are people so obsessed with the weather? In my opinion, the climate plays a major role in the way we behave.
....

2 I am sure that most of you, at some point in your lives, have considered starting your own business. However, I doubt that many of you have actually done so.
....

3 It was a dark, stormy night. Frank was alone in the wooden cabin at the top of the snow-covered mountain. The wind was howling and Frank was afraid. Suddenly, there was a strange scratching at the door.
....

4 Mason woke up to the sound of rain drumming on the rooftop. Exhausted from the previous day, he slowly got out of bed and made himself a cup of coffee and some breakfast. He decided to call in sick as he felt too weak to go to work.
....

5 All in all, adolescence can be a difficult time. But as George Bernard Shaw once said, "Life is not meant to be easy; but take courage, it can be delightful."
....

19 **a)** Match the beginnings to the endings. What types of writing are the extracts from?

BEGINNINGS...

A ☐ It was an autumn morning. Marianne, still in her pyjamas, turned on her laptop and sat at the kitchen table. Thinking of the amount of work she had to do, she sighed. "How am I ever going to get this done?"

B ☐ I am sure most of you have been influenced by an advertisement at some point in the past. In my opinion, advertising simply persuades people to buy things they don't need.

C ☐ Mr Norton is our Chemistry teacher. I'll never forget the first time we met him. He was in the school lab wearing a long, white coat, and he was about to mix two very strange-looking liquids. "Keep back, lads," he said. "This is a very dangerous experiment."

...ENDINGS

1 All in all, even though Mr Norton looks like a mad scientist, he is one of the kindest and most understanding teachers I've ever had. I am sure that if you had met him, you would agree with me.

2 It was 4 pm and she was exhausted but happy. "Well, I suppose what they say is true — The early bird catches the worm," she thought to herself as she turned off her laptop.

3 In conclusion, I think that advertising should be controlled so that consumers are not misled and persuaded to purchase goods they don't need. After all, as Alan H. Meyer, an American advertising executive, said, "The best ad is a good product."

b) In which extract(s) has each of these writing techniques been used?

- quotation ....
- proverb/saying ....
- addressing the reader directly ....
- ....
- direct speech ....

20 Read the extracts and replace the words in bold with synonymous ones from the lists.

most extraordinary, impressive, huge, comfortable

A The interior of the hotel is very **1) nice**. It has a **2) big** reception area with **3) nice** leather chairs and sofas for the guests. The **4) nicest** feature, however, is the marble fountain which was constructed at the beginning of the century.

paused, crept, whispering, peered

B Suddenly Jack heard someone **1) saying**, "At last I've found you." He **2) stopped** at the top of the stairs and **3) looked** down into the dark hallway. Just then, a young boy **4) came** out of the shadows.

UNDERSTANDING WRITING STYLE

The writing style you should use depends on the type of composition you are writing, the situation and the intended reader. Therefore, you should not use the same style of writing for every composition. The two main types of writing style are **formal** and **informal**. However, not all styles of writing fall under these categories. For example, in a letter to somebody you do not know very well or in an article for a student's magazine, the style used is neither formal nor informal, but a blend of the two, known as **semi-formal**.

FORMAL STYLE is characterised by:

- formal expressions, advanced vocabulary, longer sentences
  e.g. *Taking everything into consideration, it can be said that the facilities offered are of poor quality.*

- formal linking words/phrases (i.e. However, Nevertheless, In addition, Consequently, etc.)
  e.g. *Mobile phones are extremely useful for people who travel frequently. However, they can be dangerous.*

- no use of short forms (i.e. I'm, there's ...)
  e.g. *I would be grateful if ... (instead of: I'd be grateful if ...)*

- impersonal tone, i.e. use of the passive, no description of feelings
  e.g. *Late this evening, 20-year-old Tim McCormack was pulled to safety after being trapped under debris for more than ten hours.*

- factual presentation of the information
  e.g. *The Town Hall, constructed in the late 1800s, was seriously damaged by fire in 1909.*

INFORMAL STYLE is characterised by:

- everyday/colloquial expressions, vocabulary and idioms.
  e.g. *I thought I'd drop you a line ..., Thanks a million ..., etc*

- frequent use of short forms
  e.g. *I won't be able to come to your party as I'll be away on a business trip.*

- informal phrasal verbs
  e.g. *Lucy takes after her father. She's ...*

- simple linking words/phrases (i.e. *but, so, because, and, etc*)
  e.g. *It rains a lot here, so you'd better take an umbrella with you.*

- shorter sentences
  e.g. *Thanks a lot for the invitation. I'd love to come.*

- personal tone i.e. use of first person (I/We)
  e.g. *I've got great news. I've found a new job.*

- descriptive tone i.e. use of adjectives/adverbs etc for vivid description
  e.g. *It was a bitterly cold winter morning.*

SEMI-FORMAL STYLE

SEMI-FORMAL STYLE is characterised by:

- less formal language
- less frequent use of short forms, formal linking words/phrases or the passive
- respectful, polite tone

Compare:
> **Formal:** *I would be grateful if you could reply at your earliest convenience.*
> **Semi-formal:** *I look forward to receiving your reply as soon as possible.*
> **Informal:** *I can't wait to hear from you.*

21 Use phrases from the list to fill in the blanks in the sentences, as in the example. Then, say which are written in formal and which in informal style.

assess the suitability, porcelain-white skin, were seriously injured, drop by, am entitled to, point in favour of, with flying colours, won't be able to make it, to my mind, don't miss it

1 The purpose of this report is to ... *assess the suitability* ... of Robert Hulson for the position of Assistant Manager.
= *formal style*

2 I believe I .... a full refund.

3 Well, I've got to go now. .... when you arrive in town.

4 A .... of working from home is that one can plan one's own working schedule.

5 Two drivers .... after their cars collided on the M4 late last night.

6 Guess what! I passed all my exams ....

7 With its long, black hair, beautiful blue eyes and ....
.... , it was the most exquisite doll Mary had ever seen.

8 .... living abroad
is something everyone should experience at least once in their lives.

9 .... ! I bet it's going
to be a box-office hit!

10 I'm really sorry, but I ....
.... to your graduation party.

F Suddenly, the door opened. Tracey stared in horror as the dark figure in the doorway raised its arms over its head.

22 Read the extracts below and answer the questions that follow.

A Which is better, classical or pop music? Some people believe that classical music is superior. However, I believe that both types of music offer something different to the world of entertainment.

G *Dear Mr and Mrs Smith,*
I'm writing to thank you for the kindness you showed me during my stay with you and your family in March.

a) **What type of writing is each extract from?**

b) **Which extracts use:**

1 short forms? ....
2 factual presentation of the information? ....
....
3 everyday expressions, idioms and informal phrasal verbs? ....
4 formal expressions, advanced vocabulary and longer sentences? ....
5 formal linking words/ phrases? ....

B I would be grateful if you could attend to this matter as soon as possible. I hope to hear from you soon regarding the outcome of the situation.
Yours sincerely,
Matthew Drake

C Anyway, that's my news for now. I hope you're enjoying the holidays as much as I am. Write back soon and let me know how you're getting on.
Love,
Harry

23 **What style of writing should you use in the following situations: Write F (for formal), S (for semi-formal) or I (for informal). Why?**

a a letter of complaint to the manager of a department store

b an article for a teen magazine on the latest trends in clothes

c a letter to your friend asking him for advice on which university to attend

d a news report about an accident that happened in your town

e a letter to a former teacher of yours, thanking him for his advice

D The purpose of this report is to assess the suitability of Fairfax Eateries as caterers for the firm's annual spring party.

E The rescue team began their search for the lost skiers at dawn. The missing family was located a few hours later by a search helicopter, and they were lifted to safety. No one was injured, but they were taken to hospital suffering from the cold.

24 The extracts below are written in the wrong style. Replace the words/phrases in bold with more suitable ones from each list.

the slightest, reached, collapsed, firstly, what is more, was not

A **1) For starters,** the ironing board **2) wasn't** high enough. For example, when I unfolded it, it only **3) came up to** my waist. **4) And then**, whenever I put **5) a little bit of** pressure on the board, it **6) fell down**.

I've met, also, really love, dull moment, in common

B I **1) am enjoying myself immensely at** university. **2) I have had the opportunity to meet** many interesting people and there is never a **3) shortage of activities** on campus. **4) In addition to this**, my roommate, Becky, is a wonderful person. We have so much **5) to share** that I feel as if I've known her all my life.

what is more, however, full of comical scenes, extremely realistic, computer-generated images

C The script is simple and straightforward **1) but** it is **2) really funny**. **3) Another thing is**, all the **4) things made by the computer** are **5) lifelike** and the characters are truly convincing.

EDITING YOUR ESSAY

You should always edit your piece of writing before handing it in.
In order to do this, you should make sure:

* you have used complete sentences and that the words are in the correct order (i.e. subject, verb, object, etc).
* you have used the correct grammar (e.g. past tenses for narratives).
* you do not repeat the same words, phrases, expressions, etc.
* there are no spelling errors.
* you have used the correct punctuation. (e.g. commas, full stops, question marks, etc) [See also Appendix III]
* you have indented the paragraphs (i.e. have begun the first line of each paragraph further in from the margin).

25 Read the extract and label the underlined mistakes using the following key: S (for spelling), P (for punctuation), WW (for wrong word) or G (for grammar). Then correct the mistakes, as in the example.

1	*"Its → "It's*	5	....
2	....	6	....
3	....	7	....
4	....	8	....

P

1) "Its a party invitation," said Sue as she tore open the envelope. Paula, her sister, came 2) runing into the living room and squealed with excitement when she saw the white card. "It's from Danny," she cried. Both girls knew that Danny 3) made the 4) better birthday parties in the neighbourhood. He and his family had moved there from 5) america two years before. His father was a 6) successfull lawyer, so they lived in the nicest part of town. Danny had invited the girls to his party the previous year, but they hadn't gone. They both had had the flu and they were 7) such ill that they had had to stay in bed. They were very disappointed that they 8) hadn't been able go to the party. This time, though, would be different.

26 Put the following steps into the correct order.

A ☐ **Brainstorm** for ideas and group them into **main topics**.

B ☐ Read the **rubric** carefully and underline the **key words**. Identify the type of writing, the situation, the intended reader and the style of writing.

C ☐ Edit your essay **correcting** any spelling, punctuation, grammar, etc errors.

D ☐ Write your essay in the correct **style**, using appropriate **linking words/phrases** to join your ideas and various writing techniques to make your piece of writing interesting.

E ☐ **Plan** the layout of your essay. Make sure you have a separate paragraph for each main topic. Write a **topic sentence** for each main body paragraph.

UNIT 1 Part B Letter Writing

TYPES OF LETTERS

There are various types of letters, such as:

- **letters of application**
- **letters of complaint**
- **letters to the editor** etc.

The type of letter you should write depends on the reason for writing (i.e. to give your news, to invite somebody to a party, etc to make a complaint, to apply for a job, etc). Depending on the rubric, you may be asked to write a letter for more than one reason (i.e. to give your news and ask for advice.) The most common reasons for writing a letter are:

- giving/asking about **news**
- giving/asking for **advice**
- giving/asking for **information**
- **apologising** for something
- **thanking** someone

- **congratulating** someone
- **inviting** someone
- **accepting/refusing** an invitation
- making **suggestions** etc

1 Read the extracts (A-F) and decide what type of letter each is from (1-6). Which key words helped you decide? Underline them.

A I really hope you can come to my party. I'm sure we'll have a wonderful time.

D I received your leaflet in the post. I am very interested in the course and would be grateful if you could give me some more information.

B I'm writing to ask you what you think I should do about Robert. I'd really like your advice as he's been ...

E I have enclosed my CV. I would be grateful if you could consider my application. I look forward to hearing from you.

C I'm having a fantastic time on holiday. I went sailing yesterday and I'm going to take part in a diving competition this afternoon. I can't wait!

F I am writing to complain about the dishwasher which I purchased from your company last Monday.

1	letter of application
2	letter giving news
3	letter of invitation

4	letter asking for information
5	letter of complaint
6	letter asking for advice

2 The paragraphs in the letter below are in jumbled order. Put them into the correct order, then identify the type of letter.

A ☐ Unfortunately, I won't be able to come as I'll be at a seminar in Berlin that week. It's a pity I'll miss your big day, but I promise to make it up to you.

B ☐ Anyway, thanks again for the invitation. I wish you both all the best for the future.
Love,
Margaret

C ☐ Dear Rachel,
I'm writing to thank you very much for the invitation to your wedding. I'm really happy the two of you are finally tying the knot.

LAYOUT OF LETTERS

All letters should include the following:

a) an **appropriate greeting** (e.g. *Dear Sir/Madam, Dear Aunt Claire, Dear Mrs Baker,* etc);

b) an **introduction**, in which you write your **opening remarks** (e.g. *Hi! How are you?*) and **reason(s) for writing** (e.g. *I'm just writing to congratulate you on passing your exams, I'm writing to apologise for ... , We were thrilled to hear that ... , I was sorry to hear ...* etc);

c) a **main body**, in which you write about the specific topics of the letter in detail;

d) a **conclusion**, in which you write your **closing remarks** (e.g. *Please forgive me — it won't happen again, I promise; Looking forward to seeing you ...!, Please write soon, Take care!, Can't wait to hear from you, I'd better sign off now, That's all for now*); and

e) an **appropriate ending** (e.g. *Yours faithfully* + your full name, *Lots of love* + your first name).

WRITING STYLE IN LETTERS

The writing style you should use (i.e. **informal**, **formal** or **semi-formal**), depends on **who you are writing to**. More specifically:

- when you are writing to someone you know well (i.e. a close relative, your best friend, etc.) you should use informal style.

- when you are writing to someone you do not know, or to someone who is in authority (i.e. the manager of a hotel, a doctor, etc) you should use formal style.

- when you are writing to someone you do not know very well, or someone you want to be polite and respectful to (i.e. a friend's parents, your teacher, etc) you should use semi-formal style.

(See Appendix II for examples of each style.)

CHARACTERISTICS OF:

a) INFORMAL LETTERS

- **address & date**
  i.e. your address in the top, right-hand corner, followed by the date.

- **greeting**
  (e.g. *Dear John, Dear Mum,* etc.)

- **informal language**
  (e.g. *I've been meaning to write to you for ages; Don't worry; By the way; It was a piece of cake; I'll pick you up; We can give it a try,* etc)

- **ending**
  (e.g. *Yours/Love/Best wishes/Regards/etc + your first name*)

b) FORMAL LETTERS

- **address & date**
  i.e. your address as well as the recipient's address. Your address in the top, right-hand corner, followed by the date. The recipient's position, the name and address of the company, organisation, etc on the left-hand side.

- **greeting** (e.g. *Dear Mrs Davis* — when you know the person's name — *Dear Sir/Madam* — when you do not know the person's name)

- **formal language** (e.g. *I am writing with regard to your advertisement; I would appreciate a reply at your earliest convenience; The product which was delivered, proved to be faulty;* etc)

- **ending** (e.g. *Yours sincerely/ faithfully + your full name*)

- **Note:** when you begin with *Dear Mr/Mrs/Ms Marcus*, you should end with *Yours sincerely* + your full name. When you begin with *Dear Sir/Madam*, you should end with *Yours faithfully* + your full name.

c) SEMI-FORMAL LETTERS

- **address & date**
  i.e. your address in the top right-hand corner, followed by the date

- **greeting**
  i.e. Dear Mr/Mrs/Ms + person's surname (*e.g. Dear Mrs Marcus*)

- **semi-formal language**

- **ending**
  (e.g. *Regards/Best wishes/*etc + your first name or full name)

3 **Mark the phrases as F (for Formal) or I (for Informal).**

1 I would also appreciate some information about ... .

2 Well, I must go now ... .

3 Please accept my sincere apologies ....

4 You are cordially invited to attend ... .

5 I am writing in response to your advertisement ... .

6 Thanks for the invitation to your dinner party ... .

7 I am writing to express my strong dissatisfaction with ... .

8 I look forward to meeting you in person ....

9 Just a quick note to tell you ... .

10 I am writing to bring to your attention the ... .

11 Please do not hesitate to contact me ... .

12 I'm so sorry to hear you're having problems with ... .

13 Write back soon ... .

14 We regret to inform you that ... .

15 I won't take no for an answer ... .

4 Read the situation below and answer the questions that follow.

This is your last year at school and you are unsure of what course to take at university. You have decided to write a letter to .... , asking for advice.

a) **What style should you use if you are writing to: A** a friend? **B** your former teacher? **C** a careers advisor?

b) **First match the beginnings and endings and then say which of the people in part a) each letter is addressed to.**

BEGINNINGS...

1 Dear Karen,
Hi! How are you? I'm writing because I've no idea which course to take at university next year. I really need your advice!

2 Dear Mrs Arnold,
I hope this letter finds you well. I am writing to ask you for some advice about which course to take at university next year.

3 Dear Sir/Madam,
I am writing to enquire whether you can advise me on which course to apply for next year at university.

...ENDINGS

A Thank you for taking the time to read this letter. I look foward to hearing from you.
Best wishes,
Amy Milton

B I would be extremely grateful if you could advise me on what to do. Thank you in advance for your kind cooperation.
Yours faithfully,
Amy Milton
Amy Milton

C What do you think I should do? Please write back soon and tell me.
Love,
Amy

5 a) **Read the pairs of expressions (1-10) and the letters which follow, then choose the most suitable expression to complete each gap.**

1) Hi – just a quick note / I am writing
2) thank you very much / say thanks a lot
3) all your help / your kind assistance
4) getting ready / preparations
5) Your contribution / What you did

6) played a big part / was very important
7) making sure / ensuring
8) occasion / whole thing
9) went so well / was such a success
10) tell you how much I appreciate / thank you enough for

Dear Gavin,   **A**
1) .... to
2) .... for
3) .... with
4) .... for
the end-of-term party.
5) ....
6) ....
in 7) ....
that the 8) ....
9) ....
I can't 10) ....
.... all your hard work.
Love,
Becky

Dear Mr Conway,   **B**
1) .... to
2) .... for
3) .... with
4) .... for
the end-of-term party.
5) ....
6) ....
in 7) ....
that the 8) ....
9) ....
I can't 10) ....
.... all your hard work.
Best wishes,
Becky Jones

b) **Which letter is informal, and which letter is semi-formal? What type of letter are they?**

6 Match the beginnings to the endings, then identify what type of letter each pair is from. Finally, say whether each pair has been written in formal or informal style.

BEGINNINGS...

1 I'm writing to tell you my wonderful news ...

2 I would greatly appreciate it if you could provide me with some information regarding ...

3 Thanks a lot for your invitation. We'd love to come ...

4 I can't tell you how sorry I am that I ruined ...

5 I am writing to draw your attention to the terrible treatment I received from ...

6 I am writing to apply for the post of music teacher as advertised in ...

...ENDINGS

A Once again, I'd like to say how very sorry I am about ...

B I enclose my CV and would be glad to attend an interview at your earliest convenience.

C Well, that's all for now. Write back and tell me what you've been up to.

D Let me know if you want us to bring anything to the party. See you on the big day!

E I look forward to receiving the information and would be grateful if you could reply as soon as possible.

F I insist on a written apology. I trust this matter will receive your immediate attention.

7 Read the rubrics below and answer the questions.

A You have seen an advertisement in the local newspaper for a teaching job. Write a letter to the headmaster of the school, applying for the job.

B A friend you haven't seen for months is getting married in the summer and has invited you to the wedding. Write a letter accepting the invitation.

C You have just returned from a trip to South America. Write a letter to a friend telling him/her all about it.

D You are the secretary of a language school and have received a letter from someone interested in learning French. Write a letter in reply, informing the person about the courses offered at your school.

E You recently bought a box of your favourite breakfast cereal. On opening it, you found that the box was half empty and the remaining contents were no longer fresh. Write a letter to the manager of the cereal company complaining about it.

F Your cousin has recently won first prize in a short story competition. Write a letter congratulating them on their success.

1) What type of letter should you write for each rubric?
2) Who is going to read your letter?
3) What style should you use in each letter?
4) How would you begin and end each letter?
5) Can you suggest appropriate opening and closing remarks for each letter?

UNIT 2 Informal Letters

1 Read questions 1 to 3, then listen to the cassette and choose the correct answers. Finally, use your answers to talk about Monique's letter.

1 Who is Monique writing to?
   A a complete stranger
   B someone she knows well

2 What is her main reason for writing?
   A to tell Jackie some good news
   B to apologise for not writing sooner

3 Which of these statements are true? Tick (✓).
In her letter to Jackie, Monique ...

   A mentions her future plans ☐
   B invites Jackie to visit her ☐
   C promises to write soon ☐

   D complains about Jackie's last letter ☐
   E asks Jackie to reply soon ☐
   F sends her regards to Jackie's parents ☐

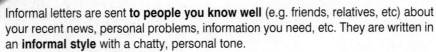

Informal letters are sent **to people you know well** (e.g. friends, relatives, etc) about your recent news, personal problems, information you need, etc. They are written in an **informal style** with a chatty, personal tone.

- An informal letter should consist of:
  a) an informal **greeting** (*Dear Ken/Aunt Joan/etc*);
  b) an **introduction** in which you write your opening remarks (i.e. asking about your friend's health, etc) and mention your reason for writing
    e.g. *Hi! How are you? I thought I'd write and let you know that ...* ;
  c) a **main body** in which you write the main subject(s) of the letter in detail, starting a new paragraph for each topic;
  d) a **conclusion** in which you write your closing remarks
    e.g. *That's all my news for now. Write back soon ...* ;
  e) an informal **ending** (e.g. *Lots of love/Best wishes/etc* + your first name).

2 Read the rubric and underline the key words, then answer the questions.

> You recently moved to a big city and have decided to write to a friend from your old neighbourhood. Write a **letter** describing life in your new city and your feelings about the change.

1 Who is going to read your letter?
2 Where is this person now?
3 Where are you now?
4 Why are you writing the letter?
5 What topics should your letter include?
6 How will you begin and end the letter?
7 Which of the following are *positive* aspects of life in a big city? Which are *negative*?
  • lots of cafés, cinemas, etc (*positive*)

  • heavy traffic (*negative*)
  • constant noise from cars
  • ugly grey buildings
  • plenty of sports facilities
  • wide choice of things to do
  • huge crowds
  • good public transport system
  • large modern shops

8 Make sentences using the prompts above and the phrases in the boxes on the right, as in the example.

Introduction

Paragraph 1

opening remarks/reason(s) for writing

Main Body

Paragraphs 2 - 3 - 4 *

development of the subject(s)

Conclusion

Final Paragraph

closing remarks

* The number of main body paragraphs may vary, depending on the rubric.

 Likes

I like living here because ...

What I like most is that there is/are ...

The best thing is that there is/are ...

 Dislikes

I hate/can't stand ...

I can't get used to ...

Unfortunately, there is/are ...

e.g. *What I like most is that there are lots of cafés and cinemas.*
I can't stand the constant noise from the cars.

9 What can you do in a big city? What can't you do? Use the prompts to make sentences, as in the examples. You can use your own ideas.

- go for a walk in the fields
- go shopping in huge shopping centres
- get around easily
- make lots of new friends
- do lots of different things
- walk home safely at night

e.g. *You can't go for a walk in the fields.*
You can go shopping in huge shopping centres.

10 Match the feelings to the reasons, then make sentences, as in the example.

1	homesick		a	the city never sleeps
2	pleased	because	b	there's more crime in the city
3	unsafe	as	c	there are always new things to do
4	disgusted		d	I miss my friends and my old neighbourhood
5	excited		e	there's rubbish everywhere

e.g. *1 d I feel homesick because I miss my friends and my old neighbourhood.*

3 **a)** **Read the letter and underline the correct tenses in bold. Then, label the paragraphs with the headings below.**

- *opening remarks/reason(s) for writing*
- *writer's feelings about the change*
- *closing remarks* • *life in the new city*

Introduction

Dear Sharon,

How are you? Sorry **1) I'm taking/I've taken** so long to write, but I've been busy settling in. Anyway, I thought **2) I'd drop/I've dropped** you a line to let you know how I'm getting on here.

Main Body

Birmingham is a really exciting city with millions of things to do. There's so much to choose from, I sometimes find it hard to make up my mind where to go! Although I still **3) didn't get/ haven't got** used to the traffic, the noise and the huge crowds, I think it's a great city.

I like living here now, but I sometimes feel homesick as I miss lots of things about Gowrie. **4) I'll never/I don't** forget the beautiful countryside and the old stone cottages. Living in the city means I can't go for long walks by the sea, either. Most of all, I miss my friends — especially you, of course! We always **5) had/were having** such a great time together, **6) haven't/ didn't** we?

Conclusion

Well, that's all my news for now. Please write back and let me know what **7) you were/you've been** up to since I **8) heard/have heard** from you last. Say "hi" to Tom and Joanna, too. I promise I'll come back and visit all of you as soon as I can.

Lots of love,

Angela

Para 1
opening remarks/ reason(s) for writing

Para 2
....
....
....

Para 3
....
....
....

Para 4
....
....
....

b) **Underline the topic sentences in the main body paragraphs, then suggest other appropriate ones.**

4 **Use the prompts to make sentences, as in the example.**

- streets are crowded — I soon got used to it (**even though**)
- lots of things to do — heavy traffic makes it difficult to get around (**however**)
- plenty of sports centres — expensive to join (**although**)

e.g. ***Even though*** *the streets are crowded, I soon got used to it.*

- not many shops — you can find almost everything you need (**but**)
- few buses and trains — always arrive on time (**nevertheless**)
- no restaurants — a few inns that serve delicious homemade food (**although**)

e.g. *There aren't many shops,* ***but*** *you can find almost everything you need.*

OPENING/CLOSING REMARKS

- **Opening remarks** in informal letters may include:
  a) questions/wishes about recent events, the person's health, etc
  b) a thank you to the person for their last letter, comments about their news
  c) an apology for a delay in writing/replying
  d) the reason why you are writing
- **Closing remarks** in informal letters may include:
  e) the reason why you must end the letter
  f) greetings to the person's family/friends
  g) wishes, a promise (e.g. to write again soon), an invitation, etc
  h) a request to the person to reply soon

5 **Match sentences 1-8 to points a-h in the box above.**

1 | a | Hello — how are you? I hope you're feeling better.
2 | b | I was sorry to hear that you aren't going to ...
3 | ☐ | I'll write as soon as I can and let you know about ...
4 | ☐ | Please write soon and tell me all your news.
5 | ☐ | Well, that's all my news. I'd better end now, because ...
6 | ☐ | The reason I'm writing is to ask you if ...
7 | ☐ | Give my best wishes to your parents.
8 | ☐ | Sorry I've taken so long to put pen to paper, but ...

INFORMAL STYLE

When writing friendly letters, you normally use informal style. Informal writing is characterised by the use of:

- everyday vocabulary (e.g. *I had a great time*)
- colloquial expressions/idioms (e.g. *drop me a line*)
- phrasal verbs (e.g. *get on, settle in*)
- short forms (e.g. *can't, don't, I'm, I'll*)

6 **Which of the following sentences are written in informal style?**

1 I'm writing to see how you're getting on in your new flat. *Informal*
2 I look forward to receiving a prompt reply.
3 Give your sister a big hug from me.
4 What are you up to this summer?
5 We're having a fantastic time here at the camp.
6 Would it be possible for you to attend the club's annual meeting next month?
7 You'd never believe how well I've been getting on at school.

7 **Some phrases in the following extracts are written in the wrong style. Read them and correct the mistakes using the words/phrases in the lists.**

ages, drop you a line, let you know, really, sorry

Dear Bob,

How are you? 1) **I apologise for the fact that** I haven't written for 2) **a considerable time**, but I've been 3) **extremely** busy. Anyway, I thought I'd 4) **communicate with you briefly** to 5) **inform you** that I've just passed my driving test!

can't wait to hear, lots of love, that's all for now, write soon, you've been up to

Well, 6) **I have no further news at present**. Please 7) **reply promptly** — I 8) **am anxious to learn** what 9) **your recent activities have been**. Take care.

10) **Yours sincerely,**

Karen

8 **Suggest opening and closing remarks for the letters below, as in the example.**

1 congratulate a friend on passing his/her exams
2 invite a friend to your birthday party
3 apologise to your friend because you couldn't go to his/her birthday party
4 ask your friend for advice on how to lose weight

e.g. 1 Opening remarks:
Hi, how's everything going? I've just heard that you passed all your exams. Congratulations!

Closing remarks:
Well, I'd better go and do some work! Once again, well done! Write soon.

9 Correct the mistakes, as in the example.

1 Congratulations ~~for~~ passing your driving test! ...*on*...

2 Write and tell me how it's like in Paris. ....

3 I still can't get used to wake up so early in the morning. ....

4 I thought I'd write and ask you to give me an advice. ....

5 I hope that everything will turn up all right. ....

6 Sorry I haven't written from ages, but I've been busy. ....

7 Write me a line and tell me all your news. ....

8 I'm writing to apologise about not coming to your wedding. ....

9 I look forward to hear from you soon. ....

10 Don't you think my news are exciting? ....

MAIN BODY PARAGRAPHS

In informal letters you usually talk about more than one topic.

- The rubric gives you information about the subject of the letter and often tells you specific topics which you <u>must</u> write about. – e.g. *You have just passed an important test or examination. Write a **letter** [2] telling a pen friend about your success and [3] describing your plans for the future.*

- These topics will be discussed in the main body of your letter. You should begin a new paragraph for each topic.

Para 1: Opening remarks
Para 2: Tell friend about success
Para 3: Describe plans for future
Para 4: Closing remarks

10 Read the rubrics below. How many main body paragraphs would each letter have? What would each paragraph be about?

A You are about to visit a friend in another country and you are not sure what clothes to take with you or how to get to their house.

e.g. **two main body paragraphs**
Para 2 – ask about clothes to take with you
Para 3 – ask how to get to friend's house

B You have recently moved into a new house. Write a **letter** to your friend describing your new house and inviting him/her to spend a weekend with you.

C Your uncle has invited you to attend his wedding in a month's time. Write a **letter** thanking him for the invitation and asking him what you should buy as a wedding present.

D You've got two tickets for a week's cruise in the Mediterranean. Write a **letter** to your friend, inviting him/her to join you, giving details of which places you are going to visit and suggestions as to what he/she will need to take with him/her.

E Your cousin is moving to your city. He/She wants to attend the same school as you. Write a **letter** to him/her, describing your school, teachers and timetable, and mentioning extra activities the school offers.

Useful expressions for making suggestions
• *I think I/you/we should ...*   • *How do you feel about + ... ing ...?*
• *Perhaps I/you/we could ...*   • *How about + ... ing ...?*
• *What do you think about + ... ing ...?*   • *Why don't I/you/we ...?*
• *What about + ... ing ...?*   • *Would you like me/us to ...?*
• *Would you like to ...?*

11 Use the prompts below and expressions from the table above to make suggestions.

1 come / dinner / my house / next Monday
2 spend / weekend / in / mountains
3 go shopping / in / city centre
4 visit / art gallery / while / be / in London

12 Look at the town map and, with a partner, suggest where and when you could meet and what you could do there.

e.g. *A: What about meeting at the Fairview Museum at noon?*
B: That's a good idea. We could admire the local art.

13 a) Read the following rubric and answer the questions.

A friend of yours, who has been living in another country for some time, is going to visit you for a week. Write a **letter** suggesting what you might do together and what sights you might visit.

1 Where would you take your friend?
2 What is the most popular attraction in your city/town?
3 Are there any bazaars, outdoor markets, fairs, restaurants, etc which are worth visiting?
4 What kind of traditional dishes would you suggest your friend should try?

b) Use your answers from questions 1 to 4 and appropriate expressions to write the main body paragraphs of this letter.

ASKING FOR ADVICE

To **ask for advice**, you can use phrases such as:
Do you think I should ...?, Should I ...?, What do you think I should do?
Do you have any idea about ...?, I'd like to know what you think about ...
Can you think of anything that ...?, I was wondering if you ...
What would you advise me to ...? etc

14 a) Read the rubric and underline the key words, then answer the questions.

You want to go on holiday in the summer but don't have enough money. Write a **letter** to a friend asking for his/her advice about ways to earn extra money.

1 Why are you writing the letter?
2 Who is going to read your letter?

3 How many paragraphs should you include in the main body?
4 Which phrases would you use to ask for advice?

b) Read the letter and underline the phrases that Mary uses to ask for advice.

Dear Pam,

Sorry that I haven't written for ages, but I've been very busy studying. I'm writing because I'd really like your advice about a problem I have.

My friends and I have decided to go away on holiday in the summer, but I don't have enough money. I was wondering if you had any ideas about earning some extra cash. If I don't save up enough money by August, I'll have to go away with Mum and Dad instead. Can you think of anything that would help me to make some money quickly?

I know that you always have lots of great ideas! What would you advise me to do? Please write back as soon as you can.

Lots of love,
Mary

GIVING ADVICE

An informal letter **giving advice** should offer sympathy and encouragement, as well as specific advice with reasons. Each piece of advice is written in a separate paragraph.

● **Opening remarks –**
I was sorry to hear that ...
Cheer up/Don't worry too much.
Don't let it get you down.
I'm only too glad to help.

- **Giving advice** —
  If I were you/in your position, I'd/ I wouldn't ...
  You should/shouldn't ...
  It would(n't)/might be a good idea (for you) to ...
  (I think) the best thing would be (for you) to ...
  Why don't you ... ?
  Have you thought of/about ... (+ -ing)?
  Another good idea is to ...

- **Result** —
  This will/would mean that ...
  Then/That way ...
  If you do this, you would ... so that you could/would ...

- **Closing remarks** —
  I hope that this/my advice helps.
  I/Let's hope that things get better/ that everything turns out all right.
  Let me know what happens.

15 Match the problems to the advice, then make sentences.

1	*b*	I can't stop eating junk food every day. I'm overweight.
2		I haven't got any friends. I'm lonely.
3		I'm very bad at Maths. I'm going to fail my exam.
4		I haven't got much money. I can't go out with my friends.
5		I argued with my friend. He/ She won't talk to me now.

a Talk to your teacher. You will get extra help.
b Join a gym. You will lose weight.
c Apologise to him/her. You'll be friends again.
d Join a club. You will meet new people.
e Get a part-time job. You will earn some money.

e.g. *Why don't you join a gym? If you do this, you'll lose weight.*

16 a) Read Pam's reply and replace phrases 1-6 with phrases A-F.

1	**A**	*I'd be happy*		**D**	*how things go*
	B	*Don't let it get you down*		**E**	*if I were you, I'd*
	C	*How about*		**F**	*Perhaps you could also*

Dear Mary,

Thanks very much for your letter, and of course 1) **I'm only too glad** to help. Here are a few things you can try to earn all the money you need.

First of all, 2) **I think you should** get a Saturday job. 3) **Have you thought of** trying to get one in a local shop so that you can be close to home? This will mean that you won't have to travel so far on Saturdays.

4) **Another good idea is to** get a job babysitting. Why don't you ask your neighbours? My only advice is not to get very young children, because they need all your attention.

I hope my advice helps. 5) **Don't give up** if you can't find a job immediately. Write and let me know 6) **what happens**.

Yours,
Pam

b) **What advice does Pam give to Mary? What other advice could you give to Mary? How else could you start and end the letter?**

17 Read the rubric, underline the key words, and answer the questions.

> Your pen friend has written you a letter asking for advice on how to improve his/her eating habits and get fit. Write a **letter** offering advice.

1 What is the reason for writing? Who is going to read your letter?
2 How many paragraphs should you include in the main body?
3 What opening and closing remarks should you write in your letter?
4 Match the advice in column A to the results in column B. Then, use appropriate expressions to make sentences, as in the example.

A	B
1 join a gym — exercise regularly	a follow balanced diet, won't put on weight
2 try not to eat so much junk food, sweets, etc	b body won't become lazy
3 eat plenty of fish, fruit and vegetables	c body won't store so much sugar and fat
4 don't go everywhere by car/bus	d soon get in shape and feel fitter

e.g. *1d If I were you, I would join a gym and exercise regularly. This will mean that you'll soon get in shape and feel fitter.*

18 Read the rubric in Ex. 17 again, then write your letter (120-180 words). Use the letter in Ex. 16 as a model, as well as your answers from Ex. 17.

UNIT 3 Formal Letters

1 a) **Read the questions below, then listen to the beginnings and endings of three letters and tick the correct box for each letter.**

	Letter 1	Letter 2	Letter 3
1 Why has the letter been written?			
A to apply for a job	☐	☐	☐
B to ask for information	☐	☐	☐
C to make a complaint	☐	☐	☐

b) **Listen again and tick the correct boxes for each letter.**

	Letter 1	Letter 2	Letter 3
2 How does the letter begin?			
A Dear Advertiser	☐	☐	☐
B Dear Sir/Madam	☐	☐	☐
C Dear Mr Williams	☐	☐	☐
3 Which of the following expressions have been used in the opening/closing remarks?			
A With reference to your advertisement ...	☐	☐	☐
B I am writing to apply for the position ...	☐	☐	☐
C I am writing to express my dissatisfaction ...	☐	☐	☐
D I look forward to hearing from you ...	☐	☐	☐
E I must insist on a full refund ...	☐	☐	☐
F Thank you in advance ...	☐	☐	☐
4 How does the letter end?			
A Yours faithfully	☐	☐	☐
B Lots of love	☐	☐	☐
C Yours sincerely	☐	☐	☐

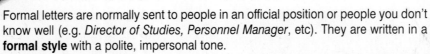

Formal letters are normally sent to people in an official position or people you don't know well (e.g. *Director of Studies, Personnel Manager*, etc). They are written in a **formal style** with a polite, impersonal tone.

- You can write a formal letter to apply for a job/course, make a complaint, give/request official information, etc.
- A formal letter should consist of:
  - **a)** a formal **greeting** (e.g. *Dear Sir/Madam - when you do not know the person's name*; *Dear Ms Green - when you know the person's name*);
  - **b)** an **introduction** in which you write your opening remarks and mention your reason(s) for writing e.g. *I am writing to apply for the position of ...*);
  - **c)** a **main body** in which you write about the main subject(s) of the letter in detail, starting a new paragraph for each topic;
  - **d)** a **conclusion** in which you write your closing remarks e.g. *I look forward to hearing from you as soon as possible ...* ;
  - **e)** a formal **ending** (*Yours faithfully - when you do not know the person's name; Yours sincerely - when you know the person's name;* + your <u>full</u> name).

Introduction
. . . .
Paragraph 1

opening remarks/
reason(s) for writing

Main Body
. . . .
Paragraphs 2 - 3 - 4 *

development of subject(s)

Conclusion
. . . .
Final Paragraph

closing remarks

* *The number of main body paragraphs may vary, depending on the rubric.*

LETTERS OF APPLICATION

When you write a letter applying for a job or a course, you should include the following information:

A) in the **opening remarks/reason(s) for writing**
- the name of the job/course, where and when you saw it advertised.
  e.g. *... the position of manager advertised in yesterday's Herald.*

B) in the **main body paragraphs** (paras 2-3-4)
- age, present job and/or studies (e.g. *I am a nineteen-year-old university student.*)
- qualifications (e.g. *I have a BA in French.*)
- experience (e.g. *I have been working as a waiter for the last two years.*)
- skills and personal qualities that are suitable for the job/course
  e.g. *I am a good and careful driver. I consider myself to be mature and responsible.*

C) in the **closing remarks**
- any other important information (i.e. when you are available for interview, where and when you can be contacted, references you can send, a remark that you hope your application will be considered, etc)
  e.g. *I will be available for interview in September.*
       I enclose references from my last two employers.
       I look forward to hearing from you.

You usually use:
   the present simple to describe skills/personal qualities
   e.g. *I am a patient and reliable person.*
   the past simple to talk about past experiences
   e.g. *I left school in 1994. I worked for General Motors for four years.*
   the present perfect to talk about recent work/studies
   e.g. *I have been working for LTYU for two years.*
       I have recently finished secondary school.

2 **Read the rubric and underline the key words, then answer the questions.**

> You saw this advertisement in a local newspaper and have decided to apply for the job.

St George's Primary School is looking for a young, energetic and experienced schoolteacher to join us in September. Must be a good organiser and keen on sports.

Please apply in writing to Mrs Hunter, giving details of qualifications, skills and previous experience and saying why you think you are suitable for the job. Closing date 12th May.

> Write your **letter of application**. Do not write any addresses.

1 Who is going to read your letter?
2 Do you know this person at all?
3 What style should you use?
4 Why are you writing this letter?
5 How should you begin and end the letter? Choose A to C.

A Dear Madam,

Yours faithfully,
Steven Davies

B Dear Headteacher,

Kind regards,
Steve

C Dear Mrs Hunter,

Yours sincerely,
Steven Davies

6 Which of the following points should you include in your letter? Tick (✓)

A your favourite subjects at school ☐
B your qualifications ☐
C your present and previous jobs ☐
D a description of your appearance ☐
E your personal qualities ☐
F your plans for the summer ☐

7 What do you think the successful candidate should be?

A patient   **D** artistic
B enthusiastic   **E** hard-working
C athletic   **F** fair

8 What experience would someone need for this kind of job?

A experience with children
B experience in public relations

9 What qualifications would someone need to apply for this job?

A a driving licence
B a BA in Education
C a degree in Media Studies
D a certificate in gymnastics
E a diploma in interior design

3 Read the letter and label the paragraphs with the headings below. Say what qualifications, experience and personal qualities Steven has. Do you think he will get the job?

- *closing remarks* • *personal qualities* • *age/present job/qualifications*
- *opening remarks/reason(s) for writing* • *experience*

Introduction

Dear Mrs Hunter,

With reference to your advertisement in Thursday's edition of the *Daily Star*, I am interested in applying for the position of primary school teacher.

Main Body

I am 28 years old and currently teaching in Margate. I have a BSc degree awarded by Glasgow University in 1997. I completed my certificate in Education at Preston Teacher Training College in 1998.

I have been working for Margate Education Department since 1999. During this time, I have enjoyed teaching a variety of subjects, including English, General Science and Games.

I consider myself to be punctual, hard-working and fair. I enjoy working with children and have good organisational skills.

Conclusion

I enclose a reference from my present employer. I would be grateful if you would consider my application. I am available for interview any weekday morning. I look forward to hearing from you.

Yours sincerely,

Steven Davies

Steven Davies

Para 1
....
....
....

Para 2
....
....
....

Para 3
....
....
....

Para 4
....
....
....

Para 5
....
....

4 Read the letter again and find formal expressions to match the informal ones in the table, as in the example.

Informal Style	Formal Style
About your advert ...	*With reference to your advertisement ...*
I want to apply for ...	....
I got my teaching certificate ...	....
I've had a job in ...	....
I think I'm always on time ...	....
I like working with kids ...	....
There's a note from my boss ...	....
I'd like it if you hired me ...	....
I'm free to talk to you ...	....
Drop me a line sometime ...	....

5 Fill in the correct form of the verbs in the list.

study, be a member, graduate, join, attend, award

1 I *graduated* from Lancers University in 1998 with a first class degree in Physical Education.

2 At the moment, I .... courses at Southfield College.

3 After leaving high school, I .... Art at the School of Fine Art in Paris.

4 I am keen on sports. I .... Barton football club three months ago.

5 I .... of the local orchestra, where I play the violin.

6 I was .... a grade A in Maths.

FORMAL STYLE

Formal style is characterised by the use of:

- **advanced vocabulary**
  e.g. *I am writing to enquire whether ... (not: I want to ask if)*
- **formal linking words/phrases**
  (*consequently, however, therefore, for this reason*)
  e.g. *I have worked as a primary school teacher for ten years and therefore have experience working with children.*
- **passive voice**
  e.g. *I can be contacted ... (not: You can contact me ...)*
- **polite forms without contractions**
  e.g. *I would be grateful if ..., I would appreciate it if you could ... I would like to apply ... (not: I'd like ...)*

Colloquial expressions, phrasal verbs, idioms and short forms are **not** used in formal style.

6 a) **Read the letters below and label the paragraphs with the headings.**

- *opening remarks/reason(s) for writing* • *experience, personal qualities*
- *closing remarks* • *age/qualifications* • *other information*

Ⓐ

Introduction

Dear Sir/Madam,

I am writing to apply for the position of part-time shop assistant which was advertised in this week's edition of the *Frankfurt English News*.

Main Body

I am a 16-year-old student. In December I passed the examination for the First Certificate in English with grade A. It is my ambition to become a teacher of English. Therefore, employment in an English-language bookshop particularly appeals to me.

Despite my lack of formal work experience, I feel that I would be well-suited for the position. For the past two years I have been a volunteer helper in our school library. In my school report I was described by the librarian as enthusiastic, dedicated and reliable.

Since the school holidays include the months of July and August, I will have no other commitments and would be available to work at any time, excluding Saturdays, for as many hours as needed.

Conclusion

I may be contacted at the above address, or by telephone on 435 1708. I look forward to receiving a reply in due course.

Yours faithfully,

Steffi Braun

Steffi Braun

Para 1
opening remarks/ reason(s) for writing

Para 2
....

Para 3
....

Para 4
....

Para 5
....

Ⓑ

Dear Manager,

Hi! **I've decided to drop you a line about the job you advertised** in the *Frankfurt English News.*

I'm a 16-year-old student, and my English isn't bad. **I got an A in the First Certificate exam! I want to be** an English teacher, so it would be lots of fun to sell English books.

I haven't worked before, but I'm sure I'd be good at the job. I've helped out in our school library for ages, and **the librarian says you can count on me to work hard.**

I won't be doing anything in July and August. We've got our school holidays then, so I can work any hours you like (but not Saturdays).

You can get in touch with me at the above address, or give me a ring on 435 1708. **Let me know soon!**

All the best,

Steffi

Steffi Braun

b) **Compare the two letters. Which one has an appropriate greeting and ending? Then, underline the phrases in Letter A which mean the same as the phrases in bold in Letter B. Which style is more suitable in a formal letter applying for a job? Why?**

c) **Read the advertisements below. Which job did Steffi apply for?**

Ⓐ
Hard-working young assistant wanted for part-time work in a bookshop during July/August. No sales experience needed, but a good understanding of English is essential.

Apply in writing to Bookworms.

Ⓑ Large department store seeking ambitious and experienced floor manager to work on a full time basis. Computer skills an asset.

For more information call J.T. Reeves at 217-3233.

7 In which letter in Ex. 6 can you find each of these features? Label each point as *A* or *B*.

1 short forms ....
2 passive voice ....
3 a friendly, personal tone ....
4 everyday vocabulary ....
5 formal linking words/phrases ....
6 phrasal verbs or idioms ....
7 longer, more complex sentences ....
8 advanced vocabulary ....
9 colloquial expressions ....
10 a polite, impersonal tone ....

8 Read the rubric, underline the key words, and answer the questions.

> You saw this advertisement in a local newspaper, and have decided to apply for the job.

> Young helpers (18 - 25) needed in our summer camp for 10 - 14 year olds. Duties include helping with games and other activities.
>
> Helpers must speak English or French and be able to work at any time, including some evenings, from 5th - 25th July. Apply in writing to Ben Carroll.

1 What skills/qualifications and personal qualities do you think would help you get the job? Circle.

- **A** energetic and sociable
- **B** can drive a car
- **C** worked in a summer camp last year
- **D** have worked as a waitress
- **E** like working with children
- **F** good at outdoor activities and sport
- **G** good cook
- **H** good organiser
- **I** speak English and French

2 Which of the points above refer to skills, qualifications, experience or personal qualities?

3 Do you know the person you are writing to?

4 What is your reason for writing?

5 How should you begin and end the letter?

9 Write your letter of application (120-180 words). Do not write any addresses. Use your answers from Ex. 8 to help you. You can use the letter in Ex. 3 as a model.

LETTERS OF COMPLAINT

In a formal letter making a complaint, you may use a **mild** tone, for complaints about minor problems, or a **strong** tone, for complaints about more serious matters, especially when you are extremely upset or annoyed. However, the language you use should never be rude or insulting.

- In the **opening remarks**, you should state your complaint, including details of what has happened and where/when the incident took place.

  e.g. (Mild)
  - *I am writing in connection with .../to complain about ... the terrible behaviour/attitude/rudeness of ...*
  - *I am writing to draw your attention to ... which ...*

  (Strong)
  - *I wish to bring to your attention a problem which arose due to your staff/inefficiency ...,*
  - *I am writing to express my strong dissatisfaction at ...*
  - *I wish to express my dissatisfaction/unhappiness with the product/treatment I received from ... on ...*

- In the **main body paragraphs**, you present each of the specific points you are complaining about. You start a new paragraph for each point and justify these points by giving examples/reasons.

  e.g.
  - *Although you advertise "top quality", I felt that the product I purchased was well below the standard I expected.*

- In the **closing remarks**, you should explain what you expect to happen (e.g. to be given a refund/replacement/apology/etc).

  e.g. (Mild)
  I hope you will replace ...
  I feel/believe that I am entitled to a replacement/refund ...
  I hope that this matter can be resolved/dealt with promptly.

  (Strong)
  I insist on/I demand a full refund/an immediate replacement/etc or I shall be forced to take legal action/the matter further.
  I hope that I will not be forced to take further action.

10 Read the rubric and underline the key words, then answer the questions.

> You recently bought a calculator, but you were given the wrong model by mistake. When you complained, the shop assistant was rude to you. Write a letter to the company's complaints department, explaining the reasons for your dissatisfaction and saying what action you expect the company to take.

1 Who is going to read your letter?

2 Do you know the person you are writing to?

3 Why are you writing this letter?

4 Would you use a mild tone or a strong tone? Why?

5 What opening and closing remarks would you write?

11 a) Read the letter opposite, and fill in the gaps with words/phrases from the list.

but also, furthermore, not only, however, in addition to, firstly, to make matters worse

b) Read the letter again and label the paragraphs with these headings.

- *closing remarks*
- *opening remarks/reason(s) for writing*
- *1st complaint & examples/reasons*
- *2nd complaint & examples/reasons*
- *3rd complaint & examples/reasons*

c) Now answer the questions.

1 Why is Mrs Adams complaining?
2 What are her specific complaints?
3 Does she justify her complaints? If so, how does she justify them?
4 What is Mrs Adams expecting? Tick (✓)

- A replacement ☐
- A full refund ☐
- The calculator to be repaired ☐
- An apology ☐

5 What will Mrs Adams do if she is not satisfied?
6 Has Mrs Adams used a mild or a strong tone? Underline the words/phrases that justify your answer.

Dear Sir/Madam,

Introduction

I am writing to express my strong dissatisfaction at the disgraceful treatment I received at the Walford branch of Stimpson's Electronics yesterday afternoon.

Para 1
....
....

Main Body

(1) .... , the product I was given was not the model I had asked for. The new X-401 calculator was demonstrated to me by the sales assistant, and I agreed to buy it. **(2)** .... , on unpacking my purchase, I saw that I had been given the smaller X-201 model instead.

Para 2
....
....

(3) .... , this calculator was much cheaper than the model I requested and paid for. It didn't have many of the features I needed and was much more basic than the one I was shown to begin with.

Para 3
....
....

(4) .... , I was deeply offended by the behaviour of the sales assistant when I went back to the shop to complain. He was **(5)** .... impolite, **(6)** .... unhelpful. He refused to contact the manager when I asked to speak to him about the incident.

Para 4
....
....

Conclusion

As you can imagine, I am extremely upset. I must insist on a full refund, **(7)** .... a written apology from the local manager, or else I shall be forced to take further action. I expect to hear from you as soon as possible.

Para 5
....
....

Yours faithfully,
Caroline Adams
Caroline Adams

---

12 Read the following extracts and say which of them are beginnings (B) and which are endings (E). What tone has the writer used in each?

1 **B** I am writing to complain about the quality of an appliance I recently purchased from your company.   mild tone

2 ☐ I demand an immediate replacement or a full refund, or I shall be forced to take the matter further. ....

3 ☐ I would appreciate it if the faulty appliance could either be replaced or repaired as soon as possible. ....

4 ☐ I am writing to inform you that I was absolutely horrified by the rudeness of your shop assistants. ....

13 Read the situations, and answer the questions that follow, as in the examples.

I A month ago you ordered some skiing equipment from a sports shop and paid by credit card. Although you asked for it to be sent by courier, you have received nothing. You urgently need this equipment.

II You recently bought an air conditioner which had been advertised on television. On receiving it, you discovered that it was nothing like the product shown in the advertisement.

III You have just come back from a package holiday where you were very disappointed by the lack of facilities and poor services.

1 Which of the following complaints would you include in each letter? Write full sentences.

A have already paid — equipment still not delivered — urgently need it *Letter I*
   ....
   ....
   ....

B contrary to advertisement — no swimming pool — rooms extremely small — no maid service ....
   ....
   ....
   ....

C model not one advertised — huge — ugly — old-fashioned model ....
   ....
   ....
   ....

2 Match the opening and closing remarks, then say which letter of complaint you would use them for.

Opening remarks ...

A I wish to express my dissatisfaction with your mail-order service.

B I am writing to express my disgust at the facilities and service offered by your travel agency.

C I feel I must complain about the misleading advertisement on TV promoting your product.

Closing remarks ...

1 I feel completely cheated and therefore demand a full refund of the money paid to you.

2 I insist that the product be replaced or else I will be forced to take further action.

3 Unless I receive the equipment by the end of this week, I will have no choice but to cancel my order.

14 Read the situation below and say:
   a) who you would address the letter of complaint to;
   b) what complaints you would include in the letter; and
   c) what opening and closing remarks you would write.

You live near a secondary school. Lately you have been disturbed by noisy children who gather outside your house, playing loud music and throwing litter into your garden.

15 Join the following complaints to their examples/reasons, using linking words/phrases from the list below, as in the example.

even though, however, in spite of the fact, nevertheless, although, but

1 The new game took fifteen minutes to load onto my computer. The salesman said it would load instantly.
   *The new game took fifteen minutes to load onto my computer, **even though** the salesman said it would load instantly.*

2 I paid for a set of five compact discs. There were only three compact discs in the box.
   ....
   ....

3 The advertisement said the tent was waterproof. Rain continually dripped into the tent.
   ....
   ....

4 The bicycle was brand new. The chain came off my bicycle the first time I rode it.
   ....
   ....

5 The battery went flat after only two hours. The instructions said it lasted for sixteen hours.
   ....
   ....

16 **Read the rubric and underline the key words, then answer the questions.**

> You recently went for a meal at Benny's fast food restaurant, which is part of an international chain. Unfortunately, the service was very slow and the food was badly cooked, so you complained to the supervisor. However, he was very rude to you and insisted on your paying for the meal. You have decided to write a letter of complaint to the company's head office. Write your **letter**, explaining the reasons for your complaint and saying what you expect the company to do.

1 What is your reason for writing?

2 Do you know the person you are writing to?

3 Would you use mild or strong language? Why?

4 How would you begin and end the letter?

5 How many main body paragraphs should you write? What should the topic of each one be?

6 Read the advertisement and the complaints in the speech bubbles. Then, use the complaints and suitable linking words/phrases to explain the reasons why you are complaining.

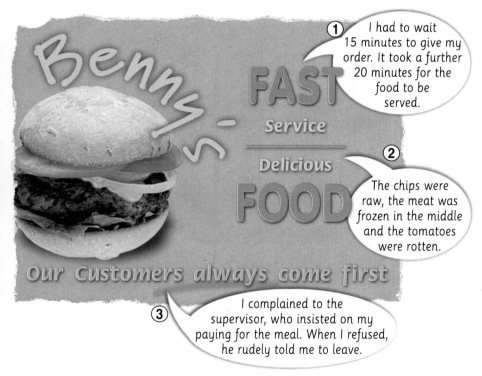

① I had to wait 15 minutes to give my order. It took a further 20 minutes for the food to be served.

② The chips were raw, the meat was frozen in the middle and the tomatoes were rotten.

③ I complained to the supervisor, who insisted on my paying for the meal. When I refused, he rudely told me to leave.

e.g. *1 **Despite** the restaurant's claim of fast service, I had to wait ...*

7 What would you expect the company to do? (e.g. refund, dismiss the supervisor, improve service, check on quality of food, etc) In which paragraph would you write your demands?

17 **These paragraphs are written in the wrong style. Correct them by using the words in the list. Then, say which is an opening remark and which is a closing remark.**

A - *as you can imagine - a full refund - a written apology - I am extremely upset - I feel I am entitled to - I look forward to receiving your prompt reply*

> 1) I'm sure you can guess 2) I'm really cross. 3) I think I should get 4) all my money back, in addition to 5) a great big "sorry" from the local manager. 6) Write soon.

B - *complained - I am writing to express - I was served - my anger - my complete dissatisfaction - the behaviour of the supervisor*

> 1) Hi — I want to tell you 2) how shocked and disgusted I was with the meal 3) I had last night at the local branch of Benny's, and 4) how really furious I was at 5) what the supervisor did when I 6) said the food was horrible.

18 **Read the rubric in Ex. 16 again. Write your letter (120-180 words), using your answers from Exs. 16 and 17 to help you. You can use the letter in Ex. 11 as a model.**

UNIT 4 Semi-formal Letters

1 Read the questions, then listen to the cassette and choose the correct answers.

1 Who is Jackie writing to?
- **A** a couple of complete strangers
- **B** people she doesn't know very well
- **C** close friends of hers

2 What style of writing does Jackie's mother say she should use?
- **A** friendly and informal
- **B** formal and official
- **C** polite and respectful

3 Which of the following does Jackie's mother say she should include? Tick (✓).
- **A** Thanks a lot for ☐
- **B** I am extremely grateful ☐
- **C** Thank you very much ☐
- **D** Yours faithfully, J M Ebdon ☐
- **E** Best wishes, Jackie Ebdon ☐
- **F** Lots of love, Jackie ☐

Semi-formal letters are sent to people you do not know very well or when you want to be more polite and respectful (e.g. a pen friend's parents, a person you do not know very well, a schoolteacher, etc). For this reason, they are written in a more polite tone than informal letters. Some formal language can be used. Compare the following:

INFORMAL   Thanks a lot for the invitation. I'd love to come to your party.

FORMAL   I would be delighted to attend your birthday celebration.

SEMI-FORMAL   Thank you for your kind invitation. I would love to join you on your birthday.

- A semi-formal letter should consist of:
  - **a)** a formal **greeting** e.g. *Dear Mr and Mrs Baker*;
  - **b)** an **introduction** in which you write your opening remarks and clearly state the reason(s) for writing, e.g. *Thank you very much indeed for your kind offer ...* ;
  - **c)** a **main body** in which you write the main subject(s) of the letter in detail, starting a new paragraph for each topic;
  - **d)** a **conclusion** in which you write your closing remarks, e.g. *I am looking forward to seeing you next month ...* ;
  - **e)** a semi-formal **ending** (*Regards/Best wishes, etc* & your **full** name).

2 Read the rubric and underline the key words, then answer questions 1 to 7.

> You are going to attend lessons at a language school in Britain. The school has arranged for you to stay with a local couple called Mr and Mrs Jackson. The Jacksons have written a letter to ask for some information. Read the extracts from their letter, then write a **letter** in reply, giving them the information they have asked for and including any questions or requests of your own.

> ... If you could send us details of your travel plans, we would be happy to meet you on arrival. We could easily come up to London ...

> Do you have any special requirements or requests regarding food? For instance, perhaps there are certain things you are not allowed to eat, or something which ...

> If there is any information you need or anything you would like us to do for you, please don't hesitate to ask. Naturally, we want ...

Introduction

Paragraph 1

opening remarks/reason(s) for writing

Main Body

Paragraphs 2 - 3 - 4 *

development of subject(s)

Conclusion

Final Paragraph

closing remark(s)

*   The number of main body paragraphs may vary, depending on the rubric.

1 Who is going to read your letter?

2 Why are you writing the letter?

3 How many main body paragraphs should you include in your letter?

4 Which of the following should you mention about your travel plans? Tick (✓).
- **a)** date and time of arrival ☐
- **b)** flight number ☐
- **c)** number of suitcases ☐
- **d)** how you will travel from the airport ☐
- **e)** cost of flight ☐

5 What could you tell them about food? Complete the following sentences:
   a) As far as food is concerned, ...
   b) The only thing(s) I don't eat is/are ....
   c) My favourite food is ....
   d) I am looking forward to trying ....

6 What questions could you ask? Think about *clothes, the weather, the town/room where you will be staying*. Then, complete the following:
   a) I was wondering if ....
   b) Perhaps you could tell me ....
   c) I would like to know ....
   d) What is .... like? Is it .... ?
   e) Do you think I need to bring .... ?

7 What opening and closing remarks could you write?

3 Read the letter and underline the words/phrases in bold which are more polite and respectful. Then, label the paragraphs with the headings below.

   • *closing remarks* • *travel plans* • *opening remarks/reason(s) for writing*
   • *food requirements* • *further questions*

Introduction

Dear Mr and Mrs Jackson,

   (1) Thanks a million/Thank you very much for your letter. **(2) I am writing/I thought I'd drop you a line** to give you the information you asked for.

Main Body

   Firstly, **(3) I'd better/I need to** tell you about my travel arrangements. I am arriving at Gatwick Airport on 14th July. My flight number is BA 451 and it lands at four thirty in the afternoon. **(4) It is very kind/It's really great** of you to offer to pick me up from London, but I have already arranged to take the train to Cardiff. Perhaps you could meet me at the station. I could phone you when I arrive.

   (5) As far as food is concerned/Now, about food, please don't go to any trouble. The only thing I don't eat is mushrooms. **(6) Anyway/Besides**, I am looking forward to trying British food.

   Finally, there are one or two things I would like to ask you. What is the weather like in Wales in August? How cold is it? Do you think I need to bring warm clothes? Also, **(7) I was wondering if you had/do you have** a computer that I could use while I am staying with you, or should I bring my laptop?

Conclusion

   Thank you once again for your letter. I am looking forward to meeting you in July.

   (8) Best wishes / Love and kisses,
   Julia Buitoni
   Julia Buitoni

Para 1
....
....
....

Para 2
....
....
....

Para 3
....
....
....

Para 4
....
....
....

Para 5
....
....
....

SEMI-FORMAL STYLE

Semi-formal style is characterised by:

• the use of less colloquial language
   e.g. *Thank you very much for your letter. (instead of: Thanks a million for your letter.)*

• less frequent use of short forms, phrasal verbs or idioms
   e.g. *I am writing to request information about ... (instead of: I thought I'd drop you a line to ask about ...)*

• a polite, respectful tone
   e.g. *I was wondering if you had ... (instead of: Do you have ...)*

4 The beginning and ending below are written in the wrong style. Read the extracts and replace the informal words/phrases in bold with more suitable semi-formal ones from each list.

I apologise for, received, Thank you for the invitation, I will be unable to visit, Mrs Ames, reply

Dear **(1) Alison,**
   (2) Thanks for asking me to your school's annual festival. I **(3) got** your letter a few weeks ago and **(4) I'm really sorry about** taking so long to **(5) write back to you**. Unfortunately, **(6) I can't come to** Hallsford on that date.

Best wishes, telephone me, any help, a great success, the preparations, don't hesitate

   Please **(7) feel free** to **(8) give me a ring** if you need **(9) a hand** with **(10) getting things ready** for the special day. I'm sure that the festival will be **(11) brilliant**.
   (12) All my love,
      Karen Smith

5 **Read the semi-formal sentences below and match them to the informal ones in the box that follows, as in the example.**

A It was very good of you to let me stay at your house.
B Could you tell me where I can get my watch repaired?
C I look forward to seeing you at the barbecue.
D I hope you find this information about bird-watching useful.
E Please accept my apology.
F I am sorry that I will be unable to attend.

		INFORMAL	SEMI-FORMAL
1	Accepting an invitation	See you at the barbecue!	C *I look forward to seeing you at the barbecue.*
2	Refusing an invitation	It's a pity that I can't come.	....
3	Thanking	Thanks again for letting me stay at your house.	....
4	Apologising	Please say you'll forgive me.	....
5	Asking for information	Do you know where I can get my watch repaired?	....
6	Giving information	Hope this was what you wanted to know about bird-watching.	....

b) **Read the beginnings and endings of the three letters (A-C) below and match them to the people (1-3) in part a).**

A ☐ Dear Mr Crowley,
I am writing to inform you of the arrangements concerning ...

... I look forward to meeting you in person during my visit.
Yours sincerely,
Suzanne Leger
Suzanne Leger

Dear Bill,
Hi! Just a quick note to let you know what I've planned about my trip ...

B ☐

... See you in a month or so. Until then, take care.

All the best,
Suzanne

C ☐ Dear Mr Richards,
I thought I should write and tell you about my travel plans ...

... I'm looking forward to meeting you while I am in London.
Best wishes,
Suzanne Leger

6 **a) You are going to London next month and must write a letter explaining your plans, so the people you are writing to can arrange to meet you. What sort of letter (*informal*, *semi-formal* or *formal*) would you write to each of these people?**

1 A businessman you have never met: ....

2 A friend you have known for several years: ....

3 A family friend who your father wants you to visit: ....

Mr C J Richards
41 Tanza Road
Hampstead
London NW3 7 IP

7 **a)** Read the rubric and underline the key words, then answer the questions.

> You have just returned from Britain, where you attended lessons at a language school. The school had arranged for you to stay with a local couple you had not met before your visit. Write a **letter** to this couple, thanking them for their kindness to you during your stay.

1 Who is going to read your letter? How well do you know these people?
2 What style should you use? Give examples.
3 Why are you writing the letter?
4 How would you begin and end the letter? Choose.

A Dear Sir/Madam,

Yours faithfully,
(full name)

B Dear Ben and Andrea,

Lots of love,
(first name)

C Dear Mr and Mrs Jackson,

Best wishes,
(full name)

D Dear friends Ben and Andrea,

Yours,
(full name)

b) Read the prompts and expand them into full sentences. Then, match them to the topic sentences of the main body paragraphs that follow.

Para 2 **A** my room / be / very comfortable, / every meal / be / delicious
....

☐ **B** what / help / me most / be / chance / practise English / you / every day
....

☐ **C** you / make me / feel like / I / be part / of / family
....

☐ **D** I / never / think / I / be able / speak / English / so well
....

> **Topic Sentences**
>
> *Para 2* – I really appreciate all your efforts that made my stay in your home a happy one.
> *Para 3* – My trip to Britain has certainly improved my English, too.

c) Choose the most suitable phrase to complete the paragraph below. Which paragraph of the letter is this?

> I am writing to tell you that I have arrived home safely, and to **(1)** ..A.. for **(2)** .... during my stay with you. **(3)** .... I **(4)** ....

1 **(A)** thank you both very much
   B say thanks a lot
   C express my gratitude to you

2 **A** all the stuff you did
   B being so kind to me
   C the kindness you displayed

3 **A** My visit was enjoyable at times, but
   B It was a wonderful experience which
   C I really had a great time, so

4 **A** am sure I will always remember.
   B won't forget in a hurry!
   C shall always have unpleasant memories of the experience.

d) Which of the phrases/ sentences below would be suitable as closing remarks? Tick (✓).

☑ **A** Thank you again for all your kindness.

☐ **B** Well, that's all my news.

☐ **C** My parents send their regards and ask me to tell you that ...

☐ **D** Mum and Dad say "Hi".

☐ **E** By the way, why don't you come and stay with us here?

☐ **F** ... you will always be welcome guests if you would like to visit my country.

☐ **G** I would love to hear from you whenever you have time to write.

☐ **H** Drop me a line sometime, won't you?

8 Read the rubric in Ex. 7 again. Write your letter (120-180 words), using your answers from Ex. 7 to help you. You can use the letter in Ex. 3 as a model.

UNIT 5 Transactional Letters

1 Look at the advertisement on the right, and the notes below. Listen to the cassette and tick the points in the notes (A-K) which have been included in the letter.

A ☐	*advert in Wessex Times, April*
B ☐	*not much information in advert*

ACTIVITIES

C ☐	*bikes - hire, or bring my own?*
D ☐	*canoeing - qualified instructor?*
E ☐	*hiking - where? - with a guide?*
F ☐	*any other activities offered?*

CHARGES, BOOKINGS, etc

G ☐	*total cost - how much?*
H ☐	*charge per day, or per activity?*
I ☐	*accommodation available?*
J ☐	*necessary to book?*

REPLY

K ☐	*write, or phone me - 0181-313-9480*

Lynwood Outdoor Centre

**canoeing
mountain biking
hiking**

For more information contact:
**Lynwood Outdoor Centre,
Lynwood House, Applegate**

Transactional letters are letters which respond to written information. This information may be in the form of advertisements, letters, invitations, notes, etc, as well as visual prompts such as maps, drawings, etc.

- Transactional letters can be of any type e.g. letters of complaint, letters of apology, letters applying for a job, letters giving/asking for information, etc.

- The style of writing can be formal, semi-formal or informal, depending on who you are writing to.

- It is important to include **all** the factual information given in the rubric. You must give this information in full sentences, using your **own words** as much as possible.
  e.g. early registration needed?
  a) *Is early registration necessary?*   c) *Do I need to register early?*
  b) *Would you recommend that*   d) *Is it necessary to register early?*
     I register early?

- You may need to summarise some information, or explain the results/importance of some facts, but you should not change the facts you are given.

2 Read the rubric and underline the key words, then answer questions 1-7.

You and two of your friends have decided to rent the cottage in the following advertisement. Read the advertisement and the notes you made after speaking to the owner. Then write a **letter** to a third friend, asking him/her to join you and giving him/her the information about the cottage and what you can do there.

1 Who are you writing to?
2 Are you going to use colloquial language? idioms? short forms? If yes, why?
3 Why are you writing the letter?
4 How would you begin and end your letter? Choose.

A	*Dear Ms Fields,*
	... Yours faithfully, + your full name
B	*Dear* + your friend's first name
	Love, + your first name

Cottage in Dorset

In beautiful countryside. Two double bedrooms, large garden. Plenty of activities & places of interest in area. Some dates still available.

Tel. 0362-211-4047 for information

Bedrooms - big, 2 beds in each
Things to do - sports centre 3 km away, horse-riding nearby
Places to visit - market, local museum, wildlife park
Price - £200 per week (i.e. £50 each)
Transport - use of 4 bikes
Dates available - 15th - 21st August

5 Which of the points below **must** you include in your letter? Tick (✓).

☐ **A** information about sleeping space

☐ **B** cooking facilities

☐ **C** activities/sports in the area

☐ **D** description of the town

☐ **E** details of the sights/tourist attractions in the area

☐ **F** the best way to get there

☐ **G** how much the holiday will cost

☐ **H** an invitation for your friend to join you

☐ **I** the telephone number of the owner

☐ **J** the dates you intend to go there

6 Complete the sentences, as in the example.

e.g. **1** *There are only two bedrooms so we'll ... .*
  A put two beds in each
  Ⓑ have to share

2 *If you join us, it's £50 each, which is a ... .*
  A bargain
  B fortune

3 *There are four bikes at the cottage which means that we can ... .*
  A visit the sports centre
  B get around easily

4 *We can rent the cottage from 15th to 21st August. So there's no need to worry about ... .*
  A the weather
  B the tourists

7 What opening and closing remarks would you write?

3 **a)** Read the letter and complete the paragraph plan using the headings below. Has Sue's letter covered all the points in the rubric, advertisement and notes? Underline the words/phrases which refer to these points.

  • persuade friend to join you • information about cottage
  • what the area offers

Dear Helen,

Introduction
Hi! How are you? I'm sorry I haven't written for ages, but I've been really busy. Anyway, I'm writing now to let you know that Claire, Jan and I have decided to rent a cottage in Dorset from 15th to 21st August and we'd love it if you could join us.

Main Body
I asked the owner all about the cottage and it sounds great. The cottage has only got two bedrooms, so we'll have to share, but the rooms are big with two beds in each. There's also a large garden. It's only £200 a week — that's £50 each, if you join us. In other words, it's a real bargain!

There are lots of things to do in the area. We can go horse-riding, and there's a sports centre not far away. There is also a market, a local museum and a wildlife park. The owner says there are four bikes at the cottage which we can use, too, which means we can get around easily.

I really hope you decide to join us. It would be such fun to go on holiday together, and the weather will probably be good at that time of the year, so I'm sure we'll all have a great time.

Conclusion
Well, that's all for now. Please write and let me know as soon as you've decided what you're going to do. Take care.

Lots of love,
Sue

	Para 1:	Opening remarks/reason(s) for writing
Main Body	*Para 2:*	....
	Para 3:	....
	Para 4:	....
	Final Para:	Closing remarks

b) Replace the topic sentences in the main body paragraphs with other appropriate ones.

REQUESTING INFORMATION

To request information you can use **direct** or **indirect questions**.
Direct questions are quite common in **informal letters** and often begin with a question word such as *what, who, when, how,* etc.
e.g. **What** *time will the party finish?* **How far** *is the hotel from the beach?*

- Most indirect questions are formed with modals such as *could, would,* etc and are normally used in semi-formal or formal letters.
  - e.g. *I* **would** *be grateful if you could tell me what time the party will finish.*
    Could *you please let me know how far the hotel is from the beach?*

- You use **if/whether** in an indirect question when there is no question word in the direct question.
  e.g. Direct question: *Do we need to bring our own food?*
  Indirect question: *I would like to know* **if/whether** *we need to bring our own food.*

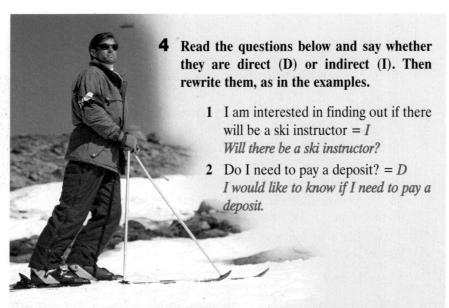

4 **Read the questions below and say whether they are direct (D) or indirect (I). Then rewrite them, as in the examples.**

  1 I am interested in finding out if there will be a ski instructor = *I*
  Will there be a ski instructor?

  2 Do I need to pay a deposit? = *D*
  I would like to know if I need to pay a deposit.

3 Could you perhaps tell me how many tickets are available?

  ....

4 I would like to know whether there are any facilities for young children.

  ....

5 What time does the play finish?

  ....

6 Do you cater for vegetarians?

  ....

7 I would appreciate it if you could send me further information.

  ....

8 Where exactly is the restaurant?

  ....

9 Could you please let me know where the nearest train station is?

  ....

10 Is the cost of equipment included in the price?

  ....

5 Look at the extracts and the notes (1-10) made about them. Then, match the notes to the sentences (a-j) opposite, as in the example.

BYDALE CAMP -
fun for all ages!
- competitive underline{prices}
- underline{English lessons daily}

1) exact cost?

2) how many hours?

3) when exactly?

ATNEX COLLEGE
Reserve a place on one of our underline{summer} courses in photography
- underline{FREE MATERIALS}

4) what do I bring?

5) marine biology books?

No matter what you want to read,
FULLSTOP BOOKSHOP
will find it for you!
- underline{ALL SCHOOL BOOKS} IN STOCK
- HUGE SELECTION OF underline{FOREIGN LANGUAGE BOOKS}

6) Portuguese?

7) lessons every day?

MIDDLETON LANGUAGE CENTRE
- underline{Intensive courses:}
  Learn Italian in three months
- 20 hours per week
- underline{Small groups} or private lessons

8) how many students?

GYMNASTICS COMPETITION
- Joolie Sports Centre
- 29th April
- underline{Tickets} still available

9) morning or afternoon?

10) how much?

40

a [1] I would appreciate it if you could let me know exactly how much the camp costs.

b [ ] Is there anything I need to bring with me?

c [ ] Could you let me know the exact dates of your courses?

d [ ] Could you please tell me how many hours per day we will have lessons?

e [ ] I'd like to know if there are classes every day.

f [ ] Do you have marine biology books?

g [ ] I would like to know if the competition takes place in the morning or afternoon.

h [ ] I would be grateful if you could tell me how much the tickets cost.

i [ ] I am interested in finding out whether you have any Portuguese books.

j [ ] I would appreciate it if you could let me know exactly how many students there are in each group.

6 a) Look at the following advertisement and write short questions about the underlined words/phrases, as in the example.

e.g. *1 Which countries?*

b) Use your short questions to write suitable sentences requesting information.

e.g. *1 I would like to know which countries I might be expected to work in.*
or *Could you please tell me which countries you operate in?*

7 a) Read the rubric below, then answer the questions.

> You are organising an end-of-term party at your school and have already made some arrangements. Read the notes you have made for a letter to your head teacher, Mrs White. Then write your **letter**, using all the information given.

Letter to Mrs White

end-of-term party —
school hall, Sat. 1st July, 8-11pm.

tell her about:

place, date, time (see above)
- who's coming (4th & 5th forms)
- music (John Smith's Disco)
- food & drink
  (Mary & Eva responsible)

ask her about:
- cost of tickets
- posters — where?

1 Should your letter:
   a give information?
   b ask for information?
   c give and ask for information?
2 Who is going to read your letter?
3 How well do you know the person?
4 How should you begin and end the letter?
5 What opening and closing remarks should you write?

b) Write sentences using the notes given.

e.g. *place/date/time: The party will be held in the school hall on Saturday 1st July from 8pm to 11pm.*

8 Read the rubric in Ex. 7 again. Write your letter (120-180 words), using your answers from Ex. 7 to help you. You can use the letter in Ex. 3 as a model.

UNIT 6 Describing People

1 **a)** Look at the photo, then listen to the cassette and label the children with their names — Martin, Ravi and Alex.

b) Listen to the cassette again and match the personal qualities to the children's names. Write **M** (for Martin), **R** (for Ravi) and **A** (for Alex). Finally, use your answers and the photograph to describe each person.

1 naughty ☐		**3** funny ☐		**5** well-behaved ☐	
2 clever ☐		**4** quiet ☐		**6** sporty ☐	

1 .... 2 .... 3 ....

A descriptive essay about a person should consist of:

a) an **introduction** in which you give general information about the person, saying when, where and how you first met them;

b) a **main body** in which you describe their physical appearance, personal qualities and hobbies/interests. You start a new paragraph for each topic;

c) a **conclusion** in which you write your comments and/or feelings about the person.

- When describing someone you know well or see often (i.e. a friend, a neighbour, etc), you should use present tenses. When describing someone who is no longer alive, or someone you knew a long time ago and you do not see any more, you should use past tenses.

- Descriptions of people can be found in articles, letters, narratives, etc. The writing style you use depends on the situation and the intended reader. For example, if you are writing an article for a magazine, you should use semi-formal style and a polite, respectful tone.

2 Read the rubric and underline the key words, then answer the questions.

The editor of your school magazine has requested articles for a special issue about friendship. You have been invited to write a short article about a close friend of yours. Write your **article** describing the person's appearance, personality and hobbies/interests.

1 Which of the following would you use? Tick (✓) or cross (✗)
passive voice ___, colloquial language ___, abbreviations ___, linking words ___, complex sentences ___

2 What tenses should you mainly use?
   A past tenses   **B** present tenses

3 Which of the following people should you *not* describe and why?
   A a historical figure   **C** your best friend
   B a film star   **D** your nursery school teacher

4 In which paragraph should you say when, where and how you first met your friend?

5 In which paragraph should you include your comments and/or feelings about your friend?

6 Which of the following main topics *must* you include? Tick (✓).

A details about his/her school timetable ☐   **D** qualifications ☐

B physical appearance & clothes ☐   **E** hobbies/interests ☐

C details about your friend's house ☐   **F** personality ☐

Introduction

Paragraph 1

name of the person when, where and how you first met him/her

Main Body

Paragraph 2

physical appearance (facial features & clothes)

Paragraph 3

personal qualities and justification(s)/examples

Paragraph 4

hobbies/interests

Conclusion

Paragraph 5

comments & feelings about the person

3 a) Use the points below to complete the table, then make sentences about your family members.

fantastic sense of humour, sailing, painting, good-looking, immature, great sense of style, scuba diving, outgoing, olive skin, curly dark hair, casual clothes, friendly, wavy hair, pale complexion, rude, lazy, pointed nose, shoulder-length hair, tall, slim, of medium height, generous, popular, skiing, bossy, attractive, plump, rafting

MAIN BODY
PARA 2 PARA 3 PARA 4

Topic	Main Points
appearance	
personal qualities	
hobbies/interests	

e.g. *My mother has a **fantastic sense of humour**.*
*My brother likes **sailing** a lot.*

b) Read the article and label the paragraphs with the headings below, then replace the topic sentences with other appropriate ones.

hobbies/interests, name & when/where/how met, comments/feelings, physical appearance & clothes, personal qualities

A Close Friend *by Jim White*

Introduction

Jacques has been my close friend for two years. I first met him on a school exchange trip to Calais, France. I asked him the way to the library and we started talking. We've been friends ever since.

Main Body

Jacques is quite good-looking. He's tall and slim, with olive skin and curly dark hair. Like many French people, he has a great sense of style, so he always looks well-dressed even in casual clothes.

Jacques is very outgoing. He is always friendly and loves to have fun. He's got a fantastic sense of humour and he always makes me laugh. However, he can be a bit immature at times. For example, when he doesn't get what he wants, he acts childishly and stamps his feet.

Jacques is very keen on water sports. He likes sailing and he spends a lot of time on his boat. He enjoys scuba diving, too, and loves exploring life under the sea.

Conclusion

All in all, I'm glad to have Jacques as my friend. It's a pleasure to be with him and I really enjoy his company. I'm sure we'll always be close friends.

Para 1
name & when/where/how met

Para 2
....
....
....

Para 3
....
....
....

Para 4
....
....
....

Para 5
....
....

• When you describe someone's **physical appearance** you start with the general features (i.e. **height**, **build**, **age**) and move on to the more specific ones, such as **hair**, **eyes**, **nose**, etc. You can also add a description of the clothes the person likes to wear.
  e.g. Laura is a tall, slim woman in her early twenties. She has got red hair, green eyes and freckles. She usually wears smart suits.

• When you describe someone's **personal qualities** you should support your description with examples and/or justifications.
  e.g. Wayne is very shy. For example, he finds it difficult to make new friends.

You can also describe someone's personality through their **mannerisms** by:
a) referring to the **way they speak**
  e.g. He speaks in a soft voice as if he were whispering.
b) describing the **gestures they use**
  e.g. She constantly uses her hands when she speaks.
c) mentioning a **particular habit they have**.
  e.g Jason always bites his nails when he is nervous.

Note: When you mention someone's negative qualities you should use mild language *(seems to, can be rather, etc)*. For example, instead of saying *Paul is lazy*, it is better to say *Paul can be rather lazy at times.*

4 Read the article in 3b) again and circle the adjectives/phrases used to describe Jacques' physical appearance and personality. Does Jacques have any negative qualities? Does the writer describe any of Jacques' mannerisms?

43

LINKING WORDS AND PHRASES

To make your piece of writing more interesting, you can use a variety of linking words and phrases to join sentences or ideas together.

e.g. Joyce has got red hair. She's got freckles.

*Joyce has got red hair **and** freckles.*
David is a tall man. He is in his late forties.

*David is a tall man **who** is in his late forties.*
Bridget is an attractive woman. She's got shoulder-length hair.

*Bridget is an attractive woman **with** shoulder-length hair.*
She is tall. She is thin.

*She is **both** tall **and** thin.*

- You can join descriptions of **similar** personal qualities by using *in addition, also, and, moreover,* etc

e.g. She is cheerful. She is always smiling. She always behaves politely.

*She is cheerful **and** is always smiling. **Moreover,** she always behaves politely.*

- You can join descriptions of **contrasting** qualities by using *but, on the other hand, however, nevertheless,* etc

e.g. He is clever and always does well at school. He can be bossy at times. *He is clever and always does well at school. **However,** he can be bossy at times.*

5 Fill in the gaps with the correct linking word/phrase from the list below.

and, but, with

1 Bob is a tall man in his late twenties .... dark hair and brown eyes. He has a beard .... he hasn't got a moustache. He likes wearing jeans, T-shirts .... trainers.

and, with, who

2 Jenny is a pretty child .... will soon be eight years old. She is quite tall for her age, ... long curly hair, big almond-shaped eyes .... a wide smile.

as well as, also, both

3 Helen is .... cheerful and friendly. She is .... polite .... kind-hearted. She never says a bad word about anyone.

however, and, also

4 Carl is very intelligent .... always gets fantastic marks in all his tests. He is .... creative and likes to write short stories. .... , Carl is rather shy and feels uncomfortable speaking in front of a lot of people.

6 a) **Look at the pictures and circle the correct item, as in the example.**

1 Susie

a   red / blonde / (dark) *hair*
b   blue / (brown) / green *eyes*
c   pointed / (small) / big *nose*

2 Mr Roberts

a   slim / medium / heavy *build*
b   young / middle-aged / elder
c   scar / beard / moustache

3 Gerald

a   short / average height / tall
b   dimples / glasses / beard
c   sportswear / business clothes / casually dressed

a   early teens / early thirties / late forties
b   wavy / curly / straight *hair*
c   fair / pale / dark *complexion*

4 Veroni

5 Julie

a   short / long / shoulder-length *hair*
b   tanned / pale / olive *skin*
c   friendly / aggressive / rude *expression*

b) Describe the people in the pictures using a variety of structures and linking words.

1 *Susie has dark hair, brown eyes and a small nose.*

2 ....

3 ....

4 ....

5 ....

7 Match the adjectives to their justifications. Then, use your answers to talk about your friends and/or relatives, as in the example.

Adjectives

1	generous	7	impatient
2	talkative	8	popular
3	energetic	9	cheerful
4	intelligent	10	lazy
5	bossy	11	well-dressed
6	rude	12	selfish

Justifications

a	*1*	always buys family presents
b		doesn't like working
c		always tells people what to do
d		wears smart clothes
e		isn't polite to other people
f		does well at school
g		is very active
h		cares only about him/herself
i		never stops chatting
j		hates waiting for anything
k		always smiles
l		is liked by everyone

My sister is a generous person who always buys her family presents.

8 Complete these descriptions using the adjectives in the list.

moody, energetic, generous, cheerful, lazy, impatient, aggressive, selfish

1 Tom is .... Whenever he visits us he brings flowers and gifts for the children.

2 Susan is .... When she gets angry she starts shouting and bangs her fist on the table.

3 Paul is .... When he has to wait for anything he constantly looks at his watch.

4 Alison is .... She hardly ever gets tired and is enthusiastic about everything.

5 My aunt Betty is .... She is always in a good mood and smiles a lot.

6 Rick is .... He doesn't like working or doing sports. He would rather sit around and watch TV all day.

7 Angela is .... She doesn't like sharing her toys with other children.

8 Wanda is .... One minute she is happy and the next she is sad and won't talk to anyone.

9 Read the paragraphs below and cross out the unnecessary words, as in the example. What is each paragraph about? How does the writer justify Megan's description? What examples of her mannerisms does the writer give?

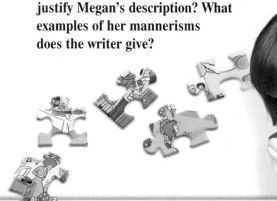

Megan is a very cheerful ~~and~~ little girl who is always happy and smiling.

However, she can ~~to~~ be a bit shy at times. Whenever she ~~will~~ meets new people she blushes then looks down at the floor.

Megan loves doing ~~the~~ puzzles. Nothing makes her ~~the~~ happier than spending ~~much~~ hours putting the pieces of a jigsaw puzzle together.

1 *and*

2 ....

3 ....

4 ....

5 ....

6 ....

10 Read the topic sentences, then write appropriate supporting sentences, as in the example.

e.g. My grandmother is a very kind-hearted person.
She cares about everyone she meets, and she is always ready to help someone in trouble.

1 Our teacher is quite handsome.
....
....
....
....

2 I like my five-year-old cousin, but he can be very naughty.
....
....
....
....

3 My friend, Jackie, is very intelligent.
....
....
....
....

4 My neighbour, Mrs Gray, takes good care of herself.
....
....
....

5 My sister's friend, Simon, loves adventure and dangerous sports.
....
....
....

11 a) Read the rubric and underline the key words. Then, read the composition and put the paragraphs into the correct order.

Your teacher has asked you to write a composition describing a person who once helped you. Write your **composition**, describing the person's appearance, personal qualities, mannerisms and hobbies/interests.

A friend in need...

A [ ] In her spare time, Ruth liked to read. She loved detective stories and crime novels, and she used to bring me many of her favourite books to read. I remember she also spoke about the karate lessons she went to twice a week.

B [ ] I first met Ruth when I was in hospital in Melbourne about three years ago. I was there on holiday, but had become seriously ill. Ruth was the patient in the next bed. She not only kept me company the whole time I was in hospital, but also visited me for many weeks after she recovered from her own illness.

C [ ] When I returned to England, we kept in touch by letter. Then, about a year ago, Ruth got a new job and moved to another part of Australia. Sadly, we have lost touch with each other, but I will never forget her kindness and help.

D [ ] Ruth had a quiet but very friendly nature. She was generous as well as kind-hearted. Whenever she visited me she always brought flowers and chocolates. She talked in a low voice because she was rather shy. She also blushed very easily, although she had a great sense of humour.

E [ ] Ruth was pretty. She was tall, fairly slim and in her mid-teens then. She had a small pretty face, with smiling eyes and long straight brown hair. She liked to dress casually in bright, colourful clothes which matched her sunny personality.

b) Have all the points in the rubric been included in the composition?

c) Which tenses have been used? Why?

d) Underline the linking words/ phrases used in the main body paragraphs.

e) What mannerisms does the writer describe in the composition?

f) Underline the topic sentences and replace them with the ones below.

1 Ruth's favourite pastime was reading.
2 Ruth was a gentle and affectionate person.
3 Ruth was quite attractive.

12 Read the rubric and underline the key words, then answer the questions.

You have seen the following advertisement in your local newspaper:

Enter our Writing Competition!

Just send us a description of a colleague or fellow student you admire, and you could win £500!

Write your **article** describing his/ her appearance, personal qualities and/or mannerisms and hobbies/interests. (120 - 180 words)

a) Which of the following people would *not* be a suitable subject for this article?
   i) a school friend ii) a relative iii) someone you work with

b) What style should you use?

c) Which tenses should you use? Why?

d) Read the following topics and decide which ones you would include in your article. Then use them to complete the plan below, as in the example.

- the person's address
- his/her hobbies/interests
- description of his/her appearance
- description of his/her job
- name, when/where/how met
- your comments/feelings
- description of the person's house
- description of his/her personality/ mannerisms

Main topics/points

Introduction	Para 1	name: *Julia Stevens* when met: *2 years ago* where met: *at work* how met: *while having a lunch break in the canteen*
Main Body	Para 2	....
	Para 3	....
	Para 4	....
Conclusion	Para 5	....

13 Read the rubric in Ex. 12 again and write your article (120-180 words). Use the plan and your answers from Ex. 12 to help you.

UNIT 7 Describing Places/Buildings

1 Look at the table below, then listen to the cassette and tick the information mentioned. Finally, use the table to describe the city.

Name:	Brussels	☐	Buenos Aires	☐	Bonn	☐
Location:	Argentina	☐	Africa	☐	Antarctica	☐
	centre of the country	☐	south-east coast	☐	north-east coast	☐
Things to see and do:	Plaza de Mayo	☐	National Gallery	☐	History Museum	☐
	Cathedral	☐	Spanish Tower	☐	Casa Rosada	☐
Shopping:	antiques fair	☐	big market	☐	superstore	☐
Nightlife:	dance halls	☐	cinemas	☐	variety of restaurants	☐
Comments:	better in August	☐	recommend it	☐	too noisy	☐

A descriptive composition about a place or building should consist of:

a) an **introduction** in which you give the name and location of the place or building and/or the reason for choosing it;

b) a **main body** in which you describe the main aspects of the place or building in detail — for example, when you describe a place you should describe what you can see and do there; when you describe a building you should describe its exterior and interior, as well as give historical facts about it;

c) a **conclusion** which includes your comments/feelings and/or a recommendation.

Descriptions of places or buildings can be found in tourist magazines, travel brochures, stories, letters, etc. The style you use depends on the situation and the intended reader. For example, in an article for a magazine you should use semi-formal style and a polite, respectful tone. You normally use **present tenses** to describe a **place/building**. You use **past tenses** to write about the historical facts.

2 Read the rubric and underline the key words, then answer the questions.

> You have seen an advertisement in an international travel magazine inviting readers to send in articles about a town they have visited. Write your **article** describing a town, including things to see and do as well as information about the town's shops and nightlife.

1 What type of writing is this? Who is going to read this? Are you going to use chatty language/abbreviations/colloquial phrases? Why (not)?

2 Which of the following points *must* you include? Tick (✓).

A	main sights	☐	**D**	entertainment	☐
B	population and climate	☐	**E**	train schedules	☐
C	shops	☐	**F**	restaurants	☐

Introduction
Paragraph 1

name, location and/or reason for choosing it

Main Body
Paragraphs 2 - 4*

main aspects in detail

[Place: things to see/do, shopping, nightlife, restaurants, etc
Building: historical facts, exterior, interior]

Conclusion
Final Paragraph

comments/feelings and/or recommendation

* The number of main body paragraphs may vary depending on the rubric.

b) Use the vocabulary from part a) and the phrases below to talk about your town, as in the example.

- The most fascinating/lively/interesting/etc part of the city is ...
- The most famous attraction is ...
- There is plenty of ...
- The town centre has ...
- The nightlife in ... is exciting, with ...
- The town is well-known for its ...

e.g. *The most interesting part of the city is the open-air market.*
The most famous attraction is the botanical gardens.

5 a) Read the article and label the paragraphs with the correct headings, then talk about Brighton.

- *comments/recommendation*
- *nightlife*
- *things to see and do*
- *name, location, reason for choosing it*
- *shopping*

PHRASES OF LOCATION

To describe the location of a place/building, you can use the following phrases.

- is situated/is located ...
- in (the) south/east/west/south-east/north-west/etc (of) ...
- on the south/east/west/north/etc coast of ...
- in the centre/heart/middle of ...

3 Look at the map, then use phrases from the table above to talk about the location of each town/city.

e.g. *Brighton is situated on the south-east coast of England.*

4 a) Match the words/phrases in the list to the headings that follow. Can you add any ideas of your own?

museum, boutique, nightclub, ancient theatre, open-air market, zoo, café, bazaar, temple, art gallery, restaurant, music hall, palace, botanical gardens, fair, theatre, souvenir shop, monument, statue, antique shop, shopping centre, amusement arcade, multi-screen cinema, funfair

Things to see and do:
Shopping:
Nightlife:

An Ideal Seaside Resort *by Sally Fulton*

Introduction

Brighton is a large town on the south-east coast of England. Located only an hour from London, it is a **charming** seaside resort and the perfect destination for a **peaceful** weekend.

Para 1
....
....

Main Body

Brighton has several tourist attractions which are worth visiting. Among these is the Royal Pavilion, a **beautiful** Indian-style palace which was built in the early nineteenth century. Brighton's most **famous** attraction is the lively Palace Pier, with its fantastic funfair and amusement arcades. Both young and old can have fun have while admiring the spectacular view of Brighton's seafront.

Para 2
....
....
....

There are plenty of places to go shopping in Brighton. The town centre has a large **modern** shopping centre. There are also **narrow** lanes full of lovely antique shops that are always bustling with tourists.

Para 3
....
....

The nightlife in Brighton is **exciting**. There are a lot of music and dance clubs which are extremely **popular** with younger people. The area is also well-known for its fashionable restaurants, which offer a variety of **international** cuisines.

Para 4
....
....

Conclusion

Brighton is a town that has something to offer everyone. Whether you want to spend your time shopping and seeing the sights, or simply relaxing and enjoying the fresh sea air, Brighton is the ideal choice for a few days away from the city.

Para 5
....
....

---

b) Underline the topic sentences in the main body paragraphs. Suggest other appropriate topic sentences.

c) Read the article in 5a) again and match the adjectives in bold with their opposites in the list below. Then, make sentences using them.

unknown, local, wide, old-fashioned, ugly, boring, unattractive, unpopular, hectic

49

USING THE SENSES

To give the reader a more vivid picture of the place/building you are describing, you can refer to the senses (i.e. sight, hearing, smell, taste and touch).
- Visitors can dine **watching the moon rise** over the mountains. (sight)
- You can **hear the sound of church bells ringing.** (hearing)
- I remember the Far East with its **aromas of exotic herbs and spices**. (smell)
- Enjoy a cup of **freshly-ground Italian coffee**. (taste)
- Relax in the **soothing warm waters** of the Roman Baths. (touch)

6 **a)** **Match the pictures (A-C) to the sentences (1-3). One of the pictures is not described. Which sense does each description refer to?**

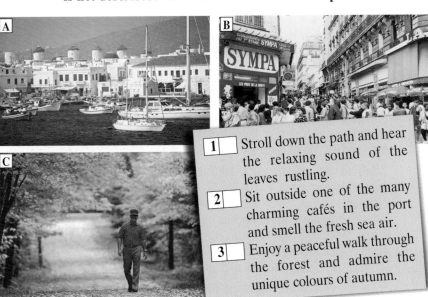

1 ▢ Stroll down the path and hear the relaxing sound of the leaves rustling.

2 ▢ Sit outside one of the many charming cafés in the port and smell the fresh sea air.

3 ▢ Enjoy a peaceful walk through the forest and admire the unique colours of autumn.

b) **Now make sentences about the picture which has not been described.**

LINKING STRUCTURES

To join short sentences you can use various linking structures. Study the examples below:
- You should visit the old part of the city. It is full of ancient temples.
  *You should visit the old part of the city, **which** is full of ancient temples.*
- Young children will enjoy the local funfair. They can go on exciting rides and eat tasty toffee-apples there.
  *Young children will enjoy the local funfair, **where** they can go on exciting rides and eat tasty toffee-apples.*
- Charlie's Lobster House is one of the most popular restaurants in the area. It has delicious lobster dishes.
  ***With** its delicious lobster dishes, Charlie's Lobster House is one of the most popular restaurants in the area.*
- Ranega Airport is on the east coast of the island. It is one of the most modern airports in the country.
  ***Situated** on the east coast of the island, Ranega Airport is one of the most modern airports in the country.*

7 **Use the words in brackets to join the sentences below.**

1 Sydney is a large and interesting city. It offers visitors a wide variety of sights to see and things to do. **(which)**

2 It is full of exotic restaurants. You can enjoy a meal there. **(where)**

3 Sydney is on the south-east coast of Australia. It has one of the busiest harbours in the country. **(located)**

4 Sydney is an ideal place for a holiday. It has a wonderful blend of cultures and friendly people. **(with)**

8 **a)** **Fill in the blanks with the correct adjectives.**

delicious, friendly, south, live, tropical, famous

- Join us in Rio in **1)** ....
  – east Brazil.
- No visit to Rio is complete without a cable car ride up Sugar Loaf Mountain!
- Why not take the train up the Corvocado to see the **2)** .... statue "Cristo Redentor"?
- Don't miss the Botanical Gardens, with almost 5,000 species of **3)** .... plants and trees.
- Have dinner at a traditional restaurant and try "feijoada" — it's **4)** ....!
- Go to a musical or a **5)** .... show.
- Learn to dance the Brazilian way at one of Rio's samba halls.
- Rio has something to offer everyone, and the people are really **6)** ....!

b) Read the rubric and underline the key words, then answer the questions.

> An international travel magazine is running a competition and has asked its readers to submit descriptions of places worth visiting. Write your **article** for the competition, describing a place and including things to see and do as well as information about nightlife there.

1 Should you use a very formal, impersonal style? Why (not)?
2 What tenses should you use?
3 Which of the points in part a) would you include in the main body of your article?
4 Read the phrases below. Which sense does each refer to? Which of these could you use in your description?
- the scent of fresh flowers
- the aroma of fresh coffee
- the blazing heat of the sun
- clear blue sky
- people talking
- cold stone floors
- spicy food
- snow-covered mountains

c) Use the information in Ex. 8a) and your answers in Ex. 8b) to help you write your article about Rio de Janeiro (120-180 words). Use the article in Ex. 5a) as a model.

9 a) Look at the table below, then listen to the cassette and tick (✓) the correct information.

Name:	Buckingham Palace	☐	Windsor Castle	☐
Location:	outside London	☐	in central London	☐
Historical Facts:	built in the 18th century	☐	built in the 8th century	☐
	official home since 1850	☐	official home since 1520	☐
Exterior:	made of marble	☐	made of iron	☐
	small windows	☐	large windows	☐
	huge balcony	☐	narrow balcony	☐
	garden with pool	☐	garden with lake	☐
Interior:	100 rooms	☐	600 rooms	☐
	red carpets	☐	red ceilings	☐
	priceless photographs	☐	priceless paintings	☐
Comment:	not to be missed	☐	not worth long queues	☐

b) Read the topic sentences, then use the information in the table to write appropriate supporting sentences.

1 In fact, the palace does not have a very long history as the home of the Royal Family.
2 From the outside, the palace is certainly impressive.
3 The interior, which can now be seen by the public, is luxuriously decorated.

DESCRIBING BUILDINGS

When you write about a building, the **main body** of the essay should include:
- a paragraph on **historical facts** about the building (when/why it was built, etc) using past tenses;
- a separate paragraph on the **exterior** (what it is made of, appearance, grounds/gardens, etc) using present tenses; and
- a paragraph on the **interior** (rooms, furniture, pictures, etc) using present tenses.

To give factual and/or historical information about the exterior and interior of a building you can also use the passive or prepositional phrases (e.g. all around, to the left, etc).

e.g. *The palace **is surrounded** by high walls.*
* **To the left** of the entrance there is a marble statue.*

10 a) Read the rubric and underline the key words, then answer the questions.

> You are a reporter for an international travel magazine. The magazine is publishing a series of articles about castles. Write an **article** describing a famous castle, including its history and a description of both the exterior and interior.

1 Who will read your article?
2 Look at the picture in part b). Which of the following would you use to describe the interior/exterior of a castle?

- swimming pool
- tall towers
- thick stone walls
- small windows

- stone floors
- modern paintings
- small attic
- glass elevator

- thick carpets
- wooden furniture
- neon lights
- huge balconies

b) Read the article and put the verbs in brackets into the correct tense, then say which verbs are active and which are passive.

An Unforgettable Castle

Bran Castle is one of the most legendary medieval castles in Europe. It **1)** .... **(situate)** high above the forest in the Carpathian mountains in Romania. Bran Castle **2)** .... **(build)** in 1212, and it was where the famous Prince Vlad Tepes once **3)** .... **(live)**. The prince and his majestic home were the inspiration for Bram Stoker's *Dracula*.

The castle is certainly an amazing sight with its breathtaking view over the countryside below. It has tall towers and thick stone walls with small windows. In medieval times, such windows **4)** .... **(make)** the castle easier to defend.

The interior is dark and gloomy. Each room has a huge fireplace and **5)** .... **(furnish)** with simple wooden items. There are no paintings on the walls, and no carpets on the cold stone floors. It looks grand, but **6)** .... **(not/design)** for comfort!

Although it may not be the typical tourist attraction, Bran Castle is certainly worth a visit. It is a truly unique experience.

c) Read the text again and complete the table below with information about the castle, then talk about Bran castle.

<table>
<tr><td rowspan="6">Main Body</td><td>Historical Facts:</td><td>*built in 1212 –* ....
....</td></tr>
<tr><td>Exterior:</td><td>...
....</td></tr>
<tr><td>Interior:</td><td>...
....</td></tr>
</table>

11 a) Fill in the boxes with words/ phrases from below.

red brick walls, tiled floor, colourful rug, well-kept garden, tall chimneys, staircase, bookshelves, wooden coffee table, little pond, large windows, leather sofas, unusual lamps, flower beds full of beautiful flowers, modern paintings

```
┌─────────────────────────┐
│        EXTERIOR         │
│                         │
│                         │
│                         │
│                         │
└─────────────────────────┘
      ( BUILDINGS )
┌─────────────────────────┐
│        INTERIOR         │
│                         │
│                         │
│                         │
│                         │
└─────────────────────────┘
```

b) Describe each of the pictures using phrases from the table above, as in the example.

e.g. There is a comfortable living room with a tiled floor.

e.g. From the outside, the building is impressive with its red brick walls.

12 a) Read the extracts. Which one is from:

- [ ] an article in a travel magazine?
- [ ] a story?
- [ ] an estate agent's advertisement?

A You will never be short of things to do in the Algarve. If you are looking for a relaxing holiday, there are plenty of long sandy beaches to choose from. For those who prefer to be on the move, there are also many pretty mountain villages where you can buy traditional Portuguese craftwork, or just admire the scenery.

B This attractive suburban home has four bedrooms, two bathrooms, a large family room with fireplace, a separate dining room and a fully-equipped kitchen. There is a small front lawn, and the back garden is fenced on three sides.

C As Donald entered the castle through a stone archway he felt as if he was in another age. A gentle wind was blowing around the old ruins. Slowly, he began to explore the area, trying to imagine how the castle had once looked.

b) Match the extracts to the pictures. One of the extracts and one of the pictures do not match.

c) Use the notes below to write part of a letter to a friend about the extra picture not described in a).

1 guess where/go/last day/our holiday
2 visit/Leaning Tower of Pisa
3 it/be/tall/eight-storey/tower
4 it/make/coloured marble
5 be/amazing sight

13 a) Read the rubric and underline the key words, then answer the questions.

> Your teacher has asked you to write a description of the most famous building in your town for the school magazine. Write your **article** including historical facts as well as describing its exterior and interior.

1 Who is going to read your article? Are you going to use abbreviations/chatty descriptions? Why/Why not?
2 How many paragraphs should you write? What should you write in each?
3 Which is the most famous building in your town/city? When was it built?
4 What kind of building is it? A church? A museum? A castle? etc
5 What is it famous for? Is it the oldest building in your town/city? Did somebody famous/important build it or live in it? etc
6 What is it used for today? A school? A library? etc
7 What does it look like from the outside? What is its inside like?
8 Is it worth visiting?
9 What topic sentences would you write for the main body paragraphs? What supporting sentences would you write for each paragraph?

b) Use your answers from part a) to write your description (120 - 180 words). You can use the article in Ex. 10b as a model.

53

UNIT 8 Describing Objects

1 Look at the table below, then listen to the cassette and tick the correct box. Which of the objects in the pictures (A-C) is being described? Use the information from the table to describe the lost object.

1 Place lost:	at the airport ☐	on the underground ☐	at the bus stop ☐
2 Time:	11:30 am ☐	11:30 pm ☐	1:30 pm ☐
3 Date:	5th December ☐	5th November ☐	6th September ☐
4 Item:	suitcase ☐	briefcase ☐	rucksack ☐
5 Size:	small ☐	medium ☐	large ☐
6 Colour:	light brown ☐	dark brown ☐	grey ☐
7 Material:	nylon ☐	plastic ☐	leather ☐
8 Special features:	shoulder strap ☐	wheels ☐	stickers ☐

A ☐

B ☐

C ☐

Descriptions of objects can be found in leaflets, catalogues, advertisements or parts of letters, stories, reports or articles.

- When you describe an object, you should give an accurate picture of it. Your description should include information about **size, weight** *(e.g. tiny, big, heavy, long, etc)*, **shape** *(e.g. circular, oval, etc)*, **pattern** or **decoration** *(e.g. plain, checked, etc)*, **colour** *(e.g. brown, multi-coloured, etc)*, **origin** *(e.g. African, Japanese, etc)* and **material** *(e.g. leather, plastic, nylon, etc)*, as well as any information concerning **special features** *(e.g. lock, stickers, etc)*.

- To describe objects you should use a variety of adjectives. Always list **opinion** adjectives *(e.g. beautiful, inexpensive, unusual, etc)* first, followed by **fact** adjectives. These are normally listed in the following order: **size/weight, age, shape, pattern, colour, origin** or **material** *(e.g. large, rectangular, silver, etc)*. Avoid using all of them one after the other, as this will make your description sound unnatural - *e.g.* Instead of writing: *It's a lovely, heavy, old, oval mirror with a carved wooden frame ...* you could write: *It's a lovely, heavy, old mirror. It's oval, with a carved frame made of wood.*

2 a) Read the extracts and match them to the types of writing in the list.

☐1 *a story*
☐2 *an advertisement*
☐3 *a letter*

Ⓐ *The last time I saw you, I forgot to tell you about the lovely new mountain bike that my dad got me for my birthday. I wish you could see it! It's quite big, but it's really light. It's got special handlebars and 18 gears. I've been going everywhere on it!*

Ⓑ With winter on the way, readers will want to take advantage of our special offer this month. It's an elegant pink and white striped quilt. Made of cotton and priced at £75, it's great value for money. To order, simply fill in the form below and send it off.

Ⓒ As she walked into the grand dining room, the first thing she noticed was the huge polished wooden table. It stretched from one end of the room to the other and it was black and shiny. Its feet were shaped like claws.

b) Underline the adjectives used to describe each object. Which are opinion adjectives? Which are fact adjectives?

54

3 **Fill in the table below with words from the list, as in the example.**

fabulous, plastic, long, elegant, straps, round, green, Chinese, striped, heavy, 20th century, crystal, light, paper, extraordinary, rectangular, ancient, purple, Irish, square, carved, stickers, modern, red, Indian, polka-dot, handmade

Opinion	*fabulous,* ....
Size/Weight	....
Age	....
Shape	....
Pattern/Decoration	....
Colour	....
Origin	....
Material	....
Special features	....

4 **a) Put the adjectives in brackets into the correct order.**

1 One of the most precious gifts I have ever received is a ....
.... mask my best friend gave me.
(Venetian, beautiful, ceramic)

2 As Mary was going through the trunks in the attic, she came across her
great-grandfather's .... radio.
(old-fashioned, wooden, carved)

3 Peter and I went to the local bazaar yesterday and we bought a ....
.... rug.
(hand-woven, fantastic, multicoloured, late 19th century)

4 Two .... deckchairs
for sale at an excellent price. Call John on 8553212 for more information.
(oak, brand-new, long)

b) Match the pictures (A-D) to the descriptions (1-4) above.

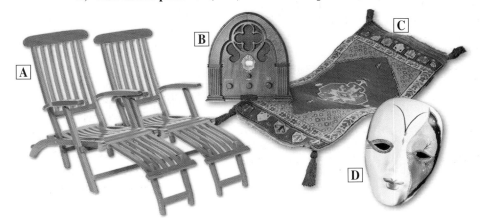

5 **a) Read the rubric and underline the key words.**

You lost a sports bag while you were staying at a hotel. You think you may have left it at the gym. Write a letter to the manager, describing the bag.

b) Tick the words/phrases that match the special features of the bag in the picture below.

zips	☐	shoulder strap	☐
wheels	☐	handles	☐
locks	☐	side pockets	☐

c) Read the letter, then write the missing paragraph describing the bag in detail. Use words/phrases from above, as well as appropriate adjectives (30-40 words).

Dear Sir/Madam,

I am writing to inquire about a bag that I think I left at your hotel on the evening of Saturday, 10th November.

....
....
....

The bag contained a pair of grey trousers and a blue tracksuit.

I would be grateful if you could inform me at your earliest convenience whether the bag has been found. I can be contacted in the mornings only on 0632 686592.

Yours faithfully,
AJ Day

UNIT 9 Describing Festivals/Events/Celebrations

1 Read the table below, then listen to the cassette and tick (✓) the information mentioned. Finally, use your answers to describe the event.

Name of festival:	La Mercé festival	☐	Sardana festival	☐
Time:	at the end of the year	☐	at the end of September	☐
Reason:	to celebrate the patron saint of Barcelona	☐	to celebrate the end of summer	☐
Preparations:	costumes made	☐	Spanish food prepared	☐
	musicians practised	☐	streets decorated	☐
Actual event:	sports events	☐	people dress up	☐
	people dancing	☐	acrobats perform tricks	☐
	lots of parades	☐	firework display	☐
Comments:	very disappointing	☐	spectacular	☐

A descriptive composition about a festival, an event or a celebration should consist of:
a) an **introduction** in which you give the name, time, place and reason(s) for celebrating;
b) a **main body** in which you describe the preparations and the actual event in separate paragraphs, using present tenses to describe annual festivals, or past tenses to describe a festival you attended at some time in the past;
c) a **conclusion** which includes people's feelings, comments or final thoughts about the event.
- You can use a variety of adjectives and adverbs to make your description more vivid. e.g. **Cheerful** fans shouted **enthusiastically** as the rock star arrived.
- You can use *the passive* to describe events when the **activity** is more important than the **agent** (i.e. the person who did it) *e.g. After the parade, speeches* **are made** *and hymns* **are sung.**

Descriptions of festivals, events or celebrations can be found in magazines, newspapers or travel brochures, or as parts of letters, stories, etc. The style you use depends on the situation and the intended reader.

2 a) Read the rubric and underline the key words, then answer the questions.

A travel magazine has asked its readers to send in descriptions of annual events in their country. Write an **article** describing an annual event you have attended, including preparations and events on the actual day.

1 Which of the following should you *not* write about? Give reasons.
  A an event held once a week in your local area
  B a festival held every year in your country
  C a ceremony that takes place every year in another country

2 Which of the following *must* you include in your description? Tick (✓).
  A detailed description of the town   C description of the actual event
  B preparations before the event   D important monuments in the area

3 Which tenses should you mainly use? Why?

Introduction
Paragraph 1
name, time/place of event, reason(s) for celebrating

Main Body
Paragraph 2
preparations
(e.g. — food, decorations, etc)

Paragraph 3
description of the actual event (e.g. — costumes, music, dancing, other activities, etc)

Conclusion
Paragraph 4
feelings, comments, final thoughts

b) Look at the picture in the article below and answer the questions.

1 What kind of event is it?
   A a boat race   **B** a carnival
2 Where do you think it takes place?
   A in England   **B** in Africa
3 What time of year is it?
   A winter   **B** summer
4 Which of the following match the picture?
   A huge grandstands alongside the water
   B exotically dressed dancers

C rows of deckchairs
D colourful tents
E elegantly dressed spectators
F boats rushing towards the finishing line
G best costume competition
H vintage cars

5 Have you ever attended an event similar to this? How did you feel? Would you like to attend such an event? Why?

c) Read the article below and put the verbs into the correct tense in the active or passive, as in the example, then match the headings below to the paragraphs.

- *description of actual event* ....
- *feelings, comments, final thoughts* ....
- *preparations* ....
- *name, place/time, reason* ....

d) Read the article again and fill in the table with your notes. Then talk about the Royal Regatta.

Para 1: ....
....
....
....
Para 2: ....
....
....
Para 3: ....
....
....
....
Para 4: ....
....
....
....

The Royal Regatta by Thomas Brown

Introduction

1 The Royal Regatta is one of the most famous events in the world of rowing. The Regatta **1)** ...*takes place*... (take place) every year in Henley, a small picturesque town in the south of England. The event **2)** .... (usually/hold) at the end of June and **3)** .... (continue) for five days. Teams of rowers from all over the globe compete for prizes, especially for the prestigious Grand Challenge Cup. Last year, I went to see what the excitement was all about.

Main Body

2 When I **4)** .... (arrive), I was amazed at the preparations involved. Huge grandstands **5)** .... (put up) alongside the water and rows of colourful deckchairs **6)** .... (place) along the edge of the river so that spectators could watch the boat race in comfort. In addition to this, tents **7)** .... (set up), in which caterers **8)** .... (serve) delicious food and refreshing drinks. Rowers from many countries **9)** .... (practise) with their team-mates for days before the races began.

3 During the five days of the Regatta, many of the spectators **10)** .... (dress) elegantly to watch the races. Others, like myself, **11)** .... (decide) to have a picnic on the river bank. The final, which is the most important race of the Regatta, was the highlight of the event. As the finalists sped towards us, everyone **12)** .... (stand up) and started shouting for their team. We cheered and **13)** .... (wave) enthusiastically as the boats **14)** .... (rush) past in their race to the finishing line. Soon afterwards, it was time for the firework display.

Conclusion

4 As the last rocket **15)** .... (explode) in the evening summer sky, I felt sad that the event was over. I couldn't help thinking how much fun it would be to learn to row like the people in the race and be more than just a spectator!

3 a) **Fill in the gaps in the extracts with adjectives from each list. Which extract describes an annual event? Which one describes a past event?**

well-known, fancy-dress, hand-carved, scary, colourful, creative

A Days before the 31st October, children go to **1)** .... shops and decide which **2)** .... costumes to buy. Others who are more **3)** .... prefer to make their own costumes. These can be anything from **4)** .... monsters to **5)** .... characters from fairy tales. Children also go trick-or-treating and make **6)** .... lanterns from pumpkins.

dim, disappointed, poor

B At the end of the concert, I felt very **1)** .... Not only was the sound quality **2)** ...., but also the lighting was so **3)** .... that we could hardly see the stage. I don't think I'll be attending next year's Rock Festival.

glamorous, glittering, lucky

C The Academy Awards, also known as the Oscars, take place once a year at the end of March in Los Angeles. This **1)** .... event is eagerly awaited by millions of fans all over the world. **2)** .... film stars, musicians and directors gather under one roof to see who will be the **3)** .... ones to take home an Oscar.

b) **Which paragraph is an introduction, a conclusion or a main body paragraph?**

4 **Rewrite the following short paragraphs, putting the verbs in bold into the passive, as in the example.**

A People **celebrate** Guy Fawkes' Day every 5th November. Children make an effigy of Guy and buy fireworks with their pocket money. People **build** big bonfires in gardens or at organised sites. In the evening, they **let off** spectacular fireworks. Everyone eats baked potatoes. At the end of the evening, they **burn** the effigy of Guy.

e.g. *Guy Fawkes' Day is celebrated every 5th November* ...

B They **display** the latest computers in a large hall and companies give away a lot of free software. They **show** full-length feature films in the auditorium. Everyone usually enjoys the event immensely.

5 **Match the beginnings and endings below. Then, say which refer to annual events, and which refer to past events. How does/did each writer feel?**

BEGINNINGS...

1 ... About three years ago, my parents organised a party in honour of my grandfather, who was retiring from work at the age of sixty-five ...

2 ... Every year, on 14th February, thousands of people in my country send each other flowers and cards to celebrate St Valentine's Day ...

3 ... Last October, for my fifteenth birthday, I invited a few of my friends to come over to my house for a party ...

...ENDINGS

A ... After I had cleared up the mess, I went to bed, exhausted but delighted that it had been such a success. I'm sure everyone will remember it for a long time.

B ... In the end, it was a great success. All the effort was worth it just to see the broad smile on his face when he was surrounded by all his family. I'll never forget it!

C ... It is usually a day full of surprises and, unavoidably, there are often disappointments. Most of all, however, it is a day for romantic people of all ages.

6 a) The prompts below are about activities that take place before and during the Dominica Carnival. Label them **B** (for before) or **D** (for during).

1 .... mouth-watering Caribbean food/sell at street stalls
2 .... brightly-decorated floats/build
3 .... local musicians/practise hard/big event
4 .... streets/fill with/people/dance and sing/ to live music
5 .... everybody/work enthusiastically/get ready/carnival
6 .... designers/make/colourful/masks/costumes
7 .... tourists/line/streets/watch/parade
8 .... night before/carnival/people go/lively street party
9 .... carnival queen/choose/award a prize

b) Use the prompts above to write the main body paragraphs for a composition describing the Dominica Carnival.

7 Listen to the cassette and tick (✓) the correct boxes, then use the table to describe the celebration. Is it an annual event or not?

Reason for celebration:	50th wedding anniversary	☐	25th wedding anniversary	☐
Place held:	hotel reception room	☐	large house	☐
Preparations:	sent invitations	☐	hired caterers	☐
	booked hotel rooms	☐	went to hairdresser's	☐
	cleaned the house	☐	ordered flowers	☐
Actual day: Guests:	50	☐	500	☐
Food:	three-course meal	☐	hot buffet	☐
Music:	Sixties	☐	Seventies	☐
Other:	party games	☐	speech	☐
Feelings:	parents had a wonderful time	☐	disappointed - some family members didn't come	☐

8 Read the rubric below and underline the key words, then answer the questions.

Your teacher has asked you to describe a wedding anniversary celebration you have recently attended. Write your **composition**, including descriptions of the preparations and the activities on the actual day.

1 Which of the following are *not* suitable for this essay? Circle.
  A 25th wedding anniversary   B wedding reception

2 Look at the activities for an anniversary celebration and label them B (for before) and D (for during).
  A make guest list   ☐
  B decide on menu   ☐
  C take photographs   ☐
  D dance to music   ☐

3 Have you ever been to a similar celebration? What was it? Who else was there? Did you have a good time? Did anything special happen?

4 Which of the following would be suitable as an introduction to your essay? Why is the other extract *not* suitable? Give reasons for your answers.

A Every anniversary is special to a married couple, but the twenty-fifth, or silver wedding anniversary is a particularly important occasion. Last Saturday was my parents' silver wedding anniversary. My brother and I organised a huge party so that Mum and Dad could celebrate the big day in style.

B The party had a really lively atmosphere. There were more than fifty guests, and later in the evening, everyone got up and danced. The DJ played my dad's favourite music from the Sixties — I've never seen him dance so much!

9 Read the rubric in Ex. 8 again, then use your answers from Exs. 7 and 8 to write your composition (120-180 words). You can use the text in Ex. 2 as a model.

UNIT 10 First-person Narratives

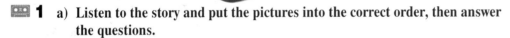

1 a) **Listen to the story and put the pictures into the correct order, then answer the questions.**

1 Who are the characters in the story?
2 Which of them is telling the story?

3 What title would you give this story?

b) **Listen again, then look at the pictures and tell the story.**

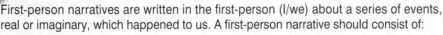

First-person narratives are written in the first-person (I/we) about a series of events, real or imaginary, which happened to us. A first-person narrative should consist of:

a) an **introduction** in which you set the scene (who was involved, time, place, etc) in an interesting way to make the reader want to continue reading;

b) a **main body**, consisting of two or more paragraphs, where you develop your story, presenting the events in the order they happened; and

c) a **conclusion** which includes what happened at the end of the story, as well as people's feelings, final comments or reactions. A surprising ending makes a long-lasting impression on the reader.

• You should normally use past tenses in such pieces of writing, as well as a variety of adjectives or adverbs to make your story more attractive to the reader. Narratives can be found in articles, letters, novels, etc. To attract the reader's attention, give interesting and catchy titles to your stories, especially if they are for a magazine, newspaper, etc.

2 **Read the rubric and underline the key words, then answer the questions.**

A local newspaper is holding a story competition and you have decided to enter. Your story should start with: *"I stood on the deck staring at the huge waves."* Write your **story** for the competition.

1 Who is going to read your story?

2 Who should your story be about?
   A your brother   B yourself

3 What should your story be about?
   A a boat trip
   B a train accident
   C a warm summer's day in the mountains

Introduction
. . . .
Paragraph 1

Set the scene
(who - where - when - what)

Main Body
. . . .
Paragraphs 2 - 4

Develop the story
detailed description of events in the order they happened

Conclusion
. . . .
Final Paragraph

end of story, feelings, comments or reactions

---

3 a) **Look at the picture in the story below and answer the questions.**

1 Where did the story take place: on a ship? on a train?
2 What was the weather like: cold and windy? warm and sunny?
3 What do you think the problem was: a hijacking? a fire in the engine room?
4 What happened in the end: the ship reached the port? the ship sank?
5 Which of the following can you find on a ship? Tick (✓):
   deck (✓), bedroom __, loudspeakers __, engine room __, platform __,
   lifeboat station __, cabin __, sitting room __, lifejackets __, bus station __

b) **Read the story and underline the correct tenses. Then, label the paragraphs with the following headings.**

- *development of story* • *setting the scene* • *end of story, feelings*

An Unforgettable Journey
by Jane Feldon

Introduction

I stood on the deck, staring at the huge waves. From the moment we **1) had left/were leaving** port and sailed into the English Channel, the weather had got worse and worse. Now, lightning flashed across the sky, which was covered in dark clouds.

Para 1
....
....

Main Body

Suddenly, the noise of the engines **2) had stopped/ stopped**. The ship **3) slowed/ was slowing**, rolling heavily in the rough sea. A voice over the loudspeakers **4) told/ were telling** us to remain calm — then added that a fire had started in the engine room, and said that all passengers must go immediately to the nearest lifeboat station.

Para 2
....
....

We all **5) ran/had run** onto the deck, following the signs to the lifeboats. The ship's officers arrived, made sure we had lifejackets and **6) showed/were showing** us how to put them on.

Para 3
....
....

I **7) looked/was looking** again in horror at the wild, stormy sea. The thought of being out there in a tiny boat was terrifying. Minutes **8) had passed/ passed** like hours, until at last a voice **9) was announcing/ announced** that everything was under control and the danger was over. We all **10) cheered/had cheered** as the engines started again and the ship **11) moved/was moving** forward into the waves.

Para 4
....
....

Conclusion

I still couldn't believe it was over, though — not until we had reached port and I **12) was standing/had stood** on solid ground again!

Para 5
....
....

c) **Read the story again and number the events in the order in which they happened. Then, use the list to retell the story as if it had happened to you.**

A		We were asked to go to the nearest lifeboat station.
B		We put on lifejackets.
C	2	A fire started in the engine room.
D		The ship slowed.
E		We reached port.
F		We went to the lifeboats.
G		The engines stopped.
H	1	The ferry left port.
I		The engines started again.

d) **Read the story again and fill in the correct adjectives, then make sentences using the completed collocations.**

1 .... waves
2 .... clouds
3 .... sea
4 .... boat
5 .... ground

Before you start writing your story you should decide on the plot line. i.e. the main events which make up the story.

You should make sure that you write these events in the order they happened. To show the sequence of events you can use linking words such as: *as soon as*, *while*, *before*, *first*, *next*, *then*, etc.

4 **a)** **Read the rubrics below and match them to the plot lines. Can you suggest alternative plot lines?**

1 A magazine is holding a competition for the best short story ending with *"We wouldn't lose our house."*

2 Your teacher has asked you to write a short story ending with *"The boy looked at me and smiled. I had saved his life."*

A
- I walked down the railway tracks.
- I saw a young boy listening to a walkman playing on the tracks.
- The train came.
- I ran towards the boy.
- I pushed him off the tracks.
- The train went by.

B
- My brother and I were looking at some bills.
- The phone rang.
- A lawyer invited us to his office.
- He told us a distant relative of ours had died.
- She left us £100,000.

b) **Read the rubric and the plot line, then put the events in the order they happened. Finally, use the plot line to tell the story as if it had happened to you.**

A magazine has asked its readers to submit short stories starting with these words. *"As soon as I got off the train I knew this would be a special day in my life."*

a	*1*	I got off the train.
b		I picked the wallet up.
c		I found the owner's address.
d		He was very happy.
e	*10*	He offered me a reward.
f		I found a wallet on the station floor.
g		I was able to buy myself a watch.
h		I gave him the wallet.
i		I went to the owner's house.
j		I opened it and looked inside.

5 **Read the extracts below and fill in the gaps with the linking words and phrases from each list.**

before, eventually, meanwhile, as soon as, suddenly, after a while

A 1) .... I arrived at the bank I joined the queue and waited for my turn. 2) ...., two men burst through the door and ran to the cashier, shouting loudly. 3) .... we knew it, the men had forced the cashier to open the security door. 4) ...., the bank manager called the police. 5) ...., we heard the police car siren blaring, but by the time they arrived, the robbers had left the building. The police chased them and 6) .... caught them.

at first, soon, suddenly, finally, then, as

B 1) .... we were driving home down the winding mountain road, it started to snow. Soft white snowflakes were falling lightly onto the road and it 2) .... became very slippery. 3) ...., a deer shot out in front of the van and I had to swerve violently to avoid it. I heard a loud thump and managed to stop. I quickly jumped out of the van and ran back to see if the deer was hurt.

I found it lying in the road. 4) ...., I thought it was dead. Then, the deer opened its eyes and I realised that it was alive. I jumped back, relieved as the deer struggled to its feet. For a moment it stood looking at me with its large soft brown eyes, 5) .... it ran off into the forest and 6) .... disappeared from view.

6 **a)** **Match the phrases below to pictures (A-D) on page 63. There is one extra picture which you do not need to use. Finally, listen to the cassette and check your answers.**

- [ ] waves thundering and crashing
- [ ] shiny green leaves
- [ ] calm water
- [ ] salty sea spray
- [ ] smell of damp ferns
- [ ] white foamy water
- [ ] sparkling lights
- [ ] loud car horns

b) **Which of the senses (i.e. sight, hearing, smell, taste and touch) have been used to describe each picture?**

PAST TENSES

You can use various past tenses in your story:

— **past simple**, to describe actions which started and ended in the past, or actions which happened one after the other in the past.
  e.g. *I went to Paris last month.*
  I walked past the bank and stopped at the post office to buy some stamps.

— **past continuous**, to set the scene or to describe events/actions in progress at a certain time in the past.
  e.g. *It was pouring with rain that evening. We were all sitting in the living room.*

— **past perfect**, for actions which happened before other past actions, or to give the background of the story. e.g. *I decided to call Mr Jones and tell him the truth about what had happened.*

7 Read the extract below and underline the correct past tense.

At first, I **1) wasn't/hadn't been** frightened by the noise as I **2) was thinking/thought** it **3) had been/was** just the wind which **4) was rattling/rattled** the windows. Then I **5) was freezing/froze** when I **6) heard/had heard** the wooden stairs creaking outside my bedroom door. I **7) was deciding/decided** to be brave and **8) went/was going** downstairs to see if it **9) had been/was** really a burglar. A few minutes later, I **10) had stood/was standing** terrified at the bottom of the stairs, looking round for a burglar. It was then that I **11) was seeing/saw** that the 'burglar' **12) was/had been** my little brother, who **13) was getting/had got up** to get a glass of water.

TECHNIQUES TO BEGIN YOUR STORY

An interesting beginning is as important as an interesting ending. An interesting beginning will catch the reader's attention and make him/her want to continue reading. A good ending will make him/her feel satisfied.

You can *START* your story by:

a) **using your senses** to set the scene and describe the weather, atmosphere, surroundings or people's actions to create mystery or suspense.
  e.g. I could hear the wind howling around me. It was quite dark that night and it felt strange to be out in the wilderness all alone.

b) **using direct speech**. *e.g. "Always look on the bright side of life, kids", Mr Frisbain used to tell us.*

c) **asking a rhetorical question**. i.e. a question that does not require an answer. *e.g. Have you ever travelled by train on a warm summer night?*

d) **addressing the reader directly**. *e.g. I am sure you all know what a bargain is.*

e) **referring to your feelings or moods**. *e.g. I was exhausted because I had been painting walls all day.*

TECHNIQUES TO END YOUR STORY

You can *END* your story by:

a) **using direct speech**. *e.g. "Thank you, sir," the boy said to me.*

b) **referring to your feelings or moods**. *e.g. We were shivering but we were happy to have made it.*

c) **asking a rhetorical question**. *e.g. "Why did I have to suffer so much?"*

d) **describing people's reactions to/feelings about the events developed in the main body**. *e.g. My brother had become the hero of the day and I was extremely proud.*

8 a) Match the beginnings to their endings.

BEGINNINGS...

1 It was a cool August night. All was quiet and peaceful in my house as my parents and two sisters were sleeping in their rooms. I was lying in bed, trying to fall asleep.

2 It was a freezing cold morning. Joanne and I were packing for our trip to Bermuda. Our flight was leaving later that afternoon. "I can't wait to enjoy the hot and sunny weather," said Joanne.

3 Aggie and I had been bored all day at school. As we wandered home, we decided to sneak into the old abandoned house at the edge of the forest. Although our parents had told us never to go in there, we couldn't resist the temptation. I am sure that you would have done the same if you had seen this house.

...ENDINGS

A Relieved to be back home, I lit the fire while Joanne unpacked our things. We both realised how lucky we had been. Without having to say anything, we understood what the other was thinking. There's no place like home, don't you agree?

B After being pulled out from under the pile of bricks, we both knew how lucky we had been. We were truly ashamed of ourselves as we glanced at the crowd waiting behind the fence, especially since our parents were there. Isn't it true that curiosity killed the cat?

C Back in my room, I felt confused and exhausted. I wasn't sure if it was a moment ago or hours ago when I had been trying to fall asleep. "I must have been dreaming," I thought to myself.

b) Which techniques have been used in each beginning and ending?

c) Write a suitable beginning and ending for a story with the title "My Worst Day".

9 a) Read the beginnings. Which one do you think is the least interesting? Why?

1 As I sat down at my desk and stared at the pile of revision notes, all I could think was, "Why me?"

2 It was a warm, sunny morning and I woke up to the sound of the phone ringing. The voice on the other end of the line simply said, "Juan, it's me. Meet me on the corner in half an hour."

3 I'm sure you all know what it's like when you have to sit an exam that you haven't studied for. Well, last May I was getting ready to ...

4 One day I went to school. On the way, I crashed my bike into a tree. The bike was badly damaged ...

5 I was really tired and was looking forward to a good night's sleep. Suddenly, I heard a strange sound coming from the garden.

b) Which of the above beginnings:

use(s) the senses	☐	☐
uses(s) direct speech	☐	☐
address(es) the reader directly	☐	☐
refer(s) to feelings or moods	☐	☐

c) Rewrite the least interesting introduction using any of the techniques mentioned.

10 **a)** **Read the rubric and underline the key words, then answer the questions.**

> A popular magazine is holding a short story competition and you have decided to enter. Your story must end with the words *"It was the best day of my life."* Write your **story**.

1 Who is going to read your story?
2 Who is the story going to be about?
3 What should your story be about?
   A a disastrous incident you'll never forget
   B your weekly routine at work
   C a day with an unexpectedly good ending

b) **Look at the pictures, then read the plot line and put the sentences into the correct order.**

— A woman stopped me.
— I waved goodbye and left.
— I arrived too late for the concert.
— I saw the woman I had helped at the entrance of the concert hall.
— I helped her change the tyre.
— She got me a front-row seat.
— I was driving to a concert.
— After the concert I met the band.
— She was the band's manager.

D

E

A

B

C

c) **Look at the pictures and use the plot line to complete the sentences below. Then, retell the story in your own words.**

• One night last year, I was on my way to see my favourite rock band.
• Suddenly, ...
   ....
• The woman thanked me, then got in her car and drove away.
• I ....
   ....
• When I arrived at the concert hall, the doors were closed.
• I was about to leave when I saw .....
   ....
• When it finished, the woman took me backstage to meet ....
   ....

11 **Read the rubric in Ex. 10 again then write your story in 120-180 words. Use your answers from Ex. 10 to help you. You can use the story in Ex. 3b as a model.**

UNIT 11 Third-person Narratives

1 The pictures below are from a story about an embarrassing incident. Try to put them in the correct order, then listen to the cassette and check your answers. Finally, look at the pictures and retell the story using the words/phrases in the list.

late, rushed, in a hurry, relieved, slight delay, embarrassed

A ☐

B ☐

C ☐

D ☐

E ☐

Third-person narratives are written in the third person (he/she/they/etc) and are real or imaginary stories about another person or other people. Like a first-person narrative, a third-person narrative should consist of:

a) an **introduction** in which you set the scene (who was involved, time, place, etc) in an interesting way to help the reader imagine the scene and want to continue reading;

b) a **main body** consisting of two or more paragraphs in which you develop your story presenting the events in the order that they happened; and

c) a **conclusion** in which you say what happened at the end and refer to people's feelings, final comments or reactions.

2 Read the rubric and underline the key words, then answer the questions.

> A popular magazine has announced a short story competition. The story must begin with the words: *"Are you sure it's safe?" Josh asked his friend.* Write your **story** for the competition.

1 Who is going to read your story?

2 Which of the following character(s) should your story be about?
   A you and your friend, Josh   **B** a man/boy called Josh and his friend

3 What should your story be about?
   A Josh's parents   **B** an accident that happened to Josh and his friend
   C Josh's autobiography

4 What should the first sentence of your story be?

Introduction
· · · · · · · · · · · · · ·
Paragraph 1

Set the scene
(who - where - when - what)

Main Body
· · · · · · · · · · · · · ·
Paragraphs 2 - 4

Develop the story
detailed description of the events in the order they happened

Conclusion
· · · · · · · · · · · · · ·
Final Paragraph

end of story, feelings, comments and reactions

3 **a) Look at the picture and answer the questions.**

1 Where were Josh and his friend Marty?
   A By a lake.   **B** On a mountain.
2 What did they want to get across?
   A A river.   **B** A mountain.
3 How did they reach the other side?
   A By climbing a fence.   **B** By walking across a rope bridge.
4 What happened when Josh began to walk on the bridge?
   A One of the ropes snapped.   **B** The wind started blowing strongly.
5 How do you think he felt?
   A Scared.   **B** Relieved.
6 What do you think happened to him in the end?
   A Marty helped him get across.   **B** He fell in the river.

b) **Read the story and find out what happened to Josh in the end. Then, label the paragraphs with the headings below. Finally, number the events in the plot line in the order they happened.**

- *end of story, feelings and comments*
- *setting the scene*
- *development of story*

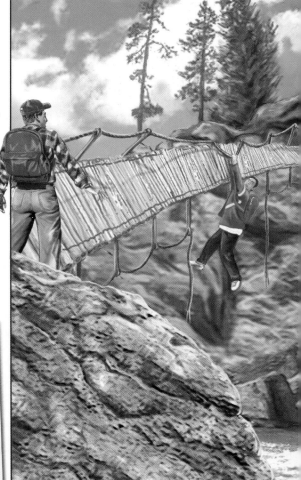

Introduction

"Are you sure it's safe?" Josh asked his friend Marty, who was just about to step onto the little rope bridge. Josh looked down at the river far beneath them and swallowed hard. Unfortunately, it was the only way to reach the other side, so he knew they had to get across before it began to get dark.

Main Body

"Look, it's as safe as houses," said Marty confidently as he put his foot onto the bridge. Once Marty was safely on the other side, Josh began to cross. The little bridge creaked under his weight, making him even more nervous than he already was. He was almost half way across the bridge when suddenly one of the ropes snapped.

Josh screamed as the bridge fell to one side, leaving him hanging over the fast-flowing river far below his feet. Terrified, he clung to the other rope. "Keep calm! Hold on!" Marty called to him. Josh looked across to where his friend stood. Slowly, hand over hand, Josh moved carefully along the rope until he was close enough for Marty to grab him.

Conclusion

Safely on the other side, Josh lay panting on the ground. He felt exhausted, but he was glad to be alive. Marty asked him if he felt he could go on. "Yes, I'm okay," he replied bravely. "We'd better go. It will be dark soon". They both set off, leaving the bridge and the terrifying incident behind them.

Para 1
....
....
....

Para 2-3
....
....
....
....
....
....
....
....
....

Para 4
....
....
....

A [3] One of the ropes snapped.
B [ ] Marty grabbed Josh.
C [ ] Josh started to cross the rope bridge.
D [ ] Marty crossed the bridge safely.
E [ ] Josh clung to the other rope.
F [ ] Marty and Josh walked away from the bridge.
G [ ] Josh moved carefully along the rope.

c) Choose the best title for the story.

a An Underwater Adventure
b An Accident in the Air
c A Nasty Experience

WRITING TECHNIQUES

To make your narrative more interesting to the reader, you should:

- use a variety of **adjectives** or **adverbs**, such as *imaginative, wonderful, cautiously, etc* instead of simplistic ones such as *nice, good, well, etc.*
  e.g. Instead of: *John is a good boy with nice ideas.*
  you can write: *John is a **great** boy with **wonderful** ideas.*

- Use a variety of **verbs** such as *wondered, screamed, whispered, etc* to avoid using "said" all the time.
  e.g. Instead of: *"Help!" he said.*
  you can write: *"Help!" he **screamed**.*

- Use **similes** i.e. expressions which describe people or things by comparing them to someone or something else.
  e.g. *She ran **like** the wind. He was **as quiet as a mouse**.*

- Use **present** or **past participles** to join two simple sentences into one longer, more sophisticated sentence.
  e.g. Instead of: *He turned on the light. He saw someone in the room.*
  you can write: ***Turning on** the light, he saw someone in the room.*
  Instead of: *She was relieved. She left the police station.*
  you can write: ***Relieved**, she left the police station.*

4 **a)** **The following adjectives or adverbs can be used instead of other simplistic ones. Put them in the correct box, as in the example.**

slight, great, evil, highly, happily, massive, delightful, extremely, successfully, horrible, miniature, tiny, remarkably, gigantic, satisfactorily, absolutely, fabulous, pleasant, huge, terrific, terrible, wicked, enormous, attractive

BIG	
SMALL	*slight*
BAD	
GOOD/NICE	
VERY	
WELL	

b) **Replace the words in the extract below with suitable ones from the boxes above.**

Melissa stepped out into the fresh and **1) nice** April morning. Her **2) good** mood brightened her **3) nice** face as she walked **4) well** to her new workplace. Upon reaching the **5) big** skyscraper, she looked up and felt **6) small**. As she entered the building, she was nervous but **7) very** excited. This job was a dream come true for her.

1 .... 3 .... 5 .... 7 ....
2 .... 4 .... 6 ....

5 **Complete the sentences with verbs from the list, as in the example.**

wondered, threatened, promised, admitted, screamed, reminded

1 "Who sent me these beautiful flowers?" Anne *wondered*, as she opened the small card attached to the bouquet.

2 "Of course I'll help you paint the cabin," Carl .... his sister when she called.

3 "Now, don't forget to pick up the tickets from the travel agents," Susan .... Bob.

4 "Run, Terry! Run faster!" Tom .... as the lion leapt over the rock.

5 "If you tell anybody what happened, I'll come after you," the man .... Dave and Ben before he drove away.

6 "Yes, I took the disc but I had no choice!" Mr Perry .... to Rachel when she saw it lying on his desk.

6 **a)** **Match Column A to Column B to complete the similes, as in the examples.**

Column A	Column B
1 as white as	**A** a leaf
2 to swim like	**B** a baby
3 to cry like	**C** a sheet
4 to run like	**D** a bee
5 as black as	**E** night
6 to shake like	**F** an ox
7 as fresh as	**G** a fish
8 as strong as	**H** a daisy
9 as busy as	**I** a sieve
10 to have a memory like	**J** the wind

e.g. *1 = C*

b) Use similes to complete the sentences, as in the example.

1 Grace dived in the sea and started swimming. She was a very good swimmer. She swam like *a fish*.
2 It was .... night inside the cave. Jeff looked for his torch.
3 She cried like .... when she heard the bad news.
4 The children were .... bees helping their parents prepare the garden for the party.
5 Sally was so scared that she was shaking like ....

7 a) Fill the correct synonym or antonym from the list. Can you think of any others to add to the table?

bored, excited, worried, scared, sure, angry, depressed

	Synonym	Antonym
thrilled	1)	disappointed
anxious	2)	relaxed
miserable	3)	glad
unsure	uncertain	4) ....
entertained	amused	5) ....
frightened	6)	unafraid
annoyed	7)	calm

b) Match the adjectives (1-6) to the feelings of the speakers (A-F). Then, make sentences in the past simple, as in the example.

1 relieved   [F]   3 worried   [ ]   5 confused   [ ]

2 amazed   [ ]   4 amused   [ ]   6 excited   [ ]

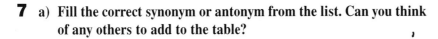

e.g. **1** *She was relieved because it was all over.*

8 a) Fill in the gaps with the correct adjective or adverb from the lists.

eagerly, beautiful, colourful, golden

A I could see the **1)**........................ sunlight streaming through the **2)** .... bedroom curtains and I knew it was going to be a **3)** .... summer's day. I lay there feeling sleepy for a moment until I suddenly remembered what day it was. **4)** ...., I jumped out of bed and got dressed. I was ready for my adventure to begin.

wonderful, warm, unbelievable, extremely

B I felt **1)** .... tired as I stepped into the **2)** .... comfortable house that I never thought I'd see again. Filled with relief that it was finally over, I tried to put the day's **3)** .... events out of my mind. Who would have guessed that a day with such a **4)** .... beginning could have turned into such a nightmare?

b) Answer the questions.

1 Which part of a story is each paragraph from?
2 How does the writer feel in each paragraph?

9 Underline the correct adverb.

1 Ellen screamed **angrily/politely** at the bus driver to move out of her way.
2 Billy spoke **rudely/casually** to the headmaster, so he was suspended from school for a week.
3 The thief crept **noisily/silently** through the house, hoping that no one would hear him.
4 The young man's hands shook **nervously/confidently** as the policeman asked to see his driving licence.
5 Before the plane took off, the passengers chatted **excitedly/miserably** about their holidays.
6 James **calmly/hurriedly** grabbed his sandwich box, kissed his mum goodbye and ran to the school bus which was already waiting outside.

10 Join the sentences using present or past participles.

1 He closed the door. He heard someone screaming.
   Closing the door, he heard someone screaming.
2 She was worried. She decided to call the local hospital.
   Worried, she decided to call the local hospital.
3 He fell to his knees. He started crying.
   ....
4 They were whispering. They walked up the stairs.
   ....
5 He was frightened. He realised no one would help him.
   ....
6 He stood at the edge of the cliff. He watched the magnificent sunset.
   ....
7 She was covered with a warm blanket. She finally felt safe.
   ....
8 She was annoyed. She gathered her things and left the room.
   ....

11 a) The following paragraphs are from a story about a journey. Put them in the correct order, then answer the questions.

A ☐ A helpful air steward helped Sharon into the icy water. Sharon was frightened because she knew the nightmare was not over yet. She started swimming towards the lights on the shore with all her strength.

B ☐ Horrified, Sharon realised that the plane was going to crash. Passengers were screaming and shouting. Sharon put her head between her knees to protect herself. There was a deafening noise as the plane crash-landed in the sea.

C ☐ She grabbed her life jacket from under her seat and pulled it over her head. The inside of the plane was dark but she managed to follow the floor lights to the exit.

1 Who is the main character of the story? Where is he/she?
2 What is happening?
3 How is he/she feeling?
4 Which part of the story are the paragraphs from?

b) Choose appropriate phrases from below to write the conclusion of the story.

- shivering with cold
- relaxed and calm
- dance the night away
- crawl onto the beach
- reach the end of the tunnel
- exhausted but relieved
- one of the happiest days in his/her life
- terrifying experience

12 a) **Read the beginnings (1 - 3) and match them with the correct endings (a - c). Which pair do you consider to be the worst? Why?**

1 [ ] Tina and her brother watched in horror as the water rose higher and higher around them. "Don't worry! I'll think of something," said Tina's brother nervously.

2 [ ] I'm sure you all know what it feels like to finally reach the end of a journey, hungry and tired, only to find that nobody is waiting for you.

3 [ ] Joe suggested that he and his friends go camping for the weekend. It seemed like a good idea.

a As I waited for the taxi driver, I looked around me one last time, hoping to see a familiar face. "Where is everyone?" I wondered.

b As the rescue worker helped them off the roof and into the boat, he said, "That was smart thinking on your part, son."

c The next morning, they took down their tents and went back home.

b) **Which writing techniques (if any) have been used in each one? Rewrite the worst pair using suitable writing techniques.**

13 a) **Look at the pictures and answer the questions.**

1

Look, Daddy! This is a great spot to spend the day.

2

1 What time of year was it?
2 Who do you think the people in the picture were?

3 What were the people doing?
4 Do you think they were having a good time?

3

Oh, my goodness! The tide is coming in!

4
You're lucky I was passing by and saw you.

5 What time do you think it was?
6 What happened?
7 Do you think they were in danger?
8 How do you think they felt?

9 Who found them?

5

10 How do you think they felt?
11 What do you think they said to the captain?

b) **Read the notes below and put the events in the order they happened. Look at the pictures, then use the notes and your answers from Ex. 13a to retell the story.**

A [ ] late afternoon — decide leave — start crossing rocks — realise — sea too far in — trapped

B [ ] Mother: "It's like paradise!" — parents sunbathe — children play and swim

C [ ] boat arrives harbour — incredibly relieved — thank captain

D [ ] hot sunny day — Hardy family — trip to seaside — find deserted beach

E [ ] see small tourist boat passing by — wave arms — boat pick them up

14 **Read the rubric and underline the key words. Then, write your essay. Use your answers to Ex. 13 to help you. You can use the story in Ex. 3b as a model.**

Your teacher has asked you to write a story which must end with the words: *"They decided to be more careful next time."* Write your **story** (120 -180 words).

UNIT 12a News Reports

📼 1 Look at the table below, then listen to the cassette and tick (✓) the information mentioned. Finally, use the table to report the event described.

Date:	Tuesday night	☐	last night	☐
Place:	island of St Finn	☐	island of Pepco	☐
Main Events:	oil tanker hit rocks	☐	oil tanker exploded	☐
	chemicals leaked into sea	☐	oil leaked into sea	☐
	seabirds, wildlife harmed	☐	seabirds, wildlife unharmed	☐
Comments and action to be taken:	beach now closed	☐	beach being cleaned	☐
	residents angry	☐	residents calm	☐
	first time faced such a situation	☐	one of worst situations ever faced	☐

News reports are short pieces of writing about current events which are of interest to the public (e.g. natural disasters, accidents, political or sports events, social events etc). They are formal and impersonal in style and they present facts accurately, objectively and unemotionally. Therefore, they do not include feelings or chatty descriptions unless these are part of someone's comments quoted in direct speech.

A news report should consist of:

a) a **short, eye-catching headline**;
b) an **introduction** which summarises the event, giving information about the time, place and people involved;
c) a **main body** consisting of two or more paragraphs in which the event is described in detail, including information about incidents and the people involved; and
d) a **conclusion** which includes people's comments on the event, action(s) to be taken and/or future developments.

News reports are found in newspapers, magazines, etc. You normally use **past tenses**, the **passive** and appropriate **reporting verbs** in this type of writing.

2 Read the rubric and underline the key words, then answer the questions.

You work for *The Bridgeton Herald* and have been asked to write a news report about a young child who received an award for bravery. Include details about the reason the award was given and information about the prize-giving ceremony.

1 Who is going to read your report?
   A your school friends
   B readers of the newspaper you work for

2 Which of the following should your article *not* be about? Give reasons.
   A a man who saved a child from drowning
   B a boy who risked his own life to save his father
   C a woman who stopped a bank robbery from taking place

Introduction
· · · · · · · · · · · · · ·
Paragraph 1

summary of the event — what/who/when/where

Main Body
· · · · · · · · · · · · · ·
Paragraphs 2, 3, 4 *

description and detailed information about event, people involved, etc

Conclusion
· · · · · · · · · · · · · ·
Final Paragraph

comments and/or actions to be taken and/or future developments

* The number of main body paragraphs may vary depending on the rubric.

3   Which of the following *must* you include in your article? Tick (✓).

A   when and where the award ceremony took place ☐

B   a description of the young child's appearance ☐

C   why the award was presented ☐

D   the weather on the day of the ceremony ☐

4   In which paragraph of your report should you give a brief summary of the event?

5   In which paragraph should you include people's comments on the event?

6   Should you use short forms? colloquial language? chatty descriptions? If so, where in your report should you use them?

3   a) **Read the news report below and label the paragraphs with the correct headings.**

- *people's comments*
- *summary of event*
- *description of ceremony*
- *reason for award*

b) **Underline the verbs in the passive. Which reporting verbs have been used in the report? In which paragraph(s) are they? Justify your answer.**

c) **Read the report again and use words from the list to complete the phrases below. Then, talk about what happened to Thomas Dakin, as in the example.**

presented, risked, came, rescue, owed, trapped, bravery, informal, saved, attended, stayed

1   was *presented* with an award
2   award for ....
3   the decision ....
4   .... his father's life
5   .... his own life
6   .... under a boulder
7   .... by his side
8   .... team
9   .... lunch
10 the event was ....
11 .... his life

e.g. *Thomas was **presented** with an award by the mayor.*

Ten-Year-Old Awarded Medal for Bravery by *Sarah White*

Introduction

A ten-year-old boy was presented with an award for bravery in a ceremony at Bridgeton Town Hall yesterday. The award was presented to Thomas Dakin by Bridgeton Mayor, John Archer.

Main Body

The decision came after Thomas saved his father's life on a hiking trip in Yorkshire last month. Thomas risked his own life to free his father, Neil Dakin, 33, who was trapped under a heavy boulder during a rock fall. Thomas called for help on his father's mobile phone and stayed by his side for five hours until the rescue team arrived.

The award ceremony began at 11:00 yesterday morning with a speech from the mayor, who congratulated Thomas and presented him with the medal. This was followed by an informal lunch in the town hall's Kilburn Suite. The event was attended by members of the council and Thomas' family.

Conclusion

Neil Dakin, now fully recovered, commented that he was delighted his son's bravery had been recognised, saying that he owed his life to him. Mayor John Archer pointed out, "Thomas is an example to us all. Everyone in Bridgeton is very proud of him."

Para 1
summary of event

Para 2
....
....
....

Para 3
....
....
....

Para 4
....
....
....

A **headline** is a short summary of what the report is about. To write a headline:
- use the **present simple** for **recent events**:
  FACTORY EXPLOSION **DAMAGES** TOWN (=has damaged/damaged)
- use **to-infinitive** to describe a **future event**: LOCAL FOOTBALL TEAM **TO FLY** TO ITALY FOR CHAMPIONS' LEAGUE (= is going to fly)
- use **to be + past participle** when using the passive voice to describe a future event: TEACHERS' ANNUAL MEETING **TO BE HELD** IN AUGUST (= is going to be held)
- use abbreviations like UK, USA, UNESCO
  UN RESCUES HOSTAGES IN SIERRA LEONE
- omit full stops or commas, articles, pronouns, auxiliary verbs and words easily understood from context: SEVEN INJURED IN TRAIN CRASH (= Seven **people were** injured in **a** train crash.)
- omit the verb "to be" when using the passive to describe a past event: YOUNG GIRL **SAVED** BY RESCUE WORKERS (= was saved)

4 Change the sentences into headlines, as in the example.

1 A bomb was found on a train which was heading for London yesterday morning. Bomb found on train heading for London
2 Many fans were injured at the football match.
   ....
3 A sixty-year-old man has been shot by some car thieves.
   ....
4 A team of local climbers reached the top of Mount Everest at three o'clock yesterday afternoon.
   ....
5 This has been a brilliant season for Manchester United football club.
   ....
6 A young girl rescued her brother from some kidnappers.
   ....

5 a) Match the headlines to the paragraphs. There is one extra headline.

a **"MISSING" TWINS FINALLY FOUND**

b **FANS INJURED AT MATCH**

c **VOLCANO CAUSES WAVES**

d **FARMER WINS £2m ON NATIONAL LOTTERY**

[1] Long-lost twin sisters Lucy Wells and Lily Summers met yesterday for the first time, thirty years after having been separated at birth.
[2] Ron Dudd, a 45-year-old farmer from Brumsville, has won two million pounds on the National Lottery.
[3] Scientists on a research ship in the Pacific Ocean had a surprise yesterday when an underwater crater suddenly erupted, causing 20-metre waves.

b) Write a suitable introduction for the headline which has not been used.

6 Use the notes to write beginnings for the following news reports. Then, give a headline for each.

1
- valuable Renoir painting
- steal late last night
- Terrence Wagner Museum
- worth over 2 million pounds
- in museum since 1983

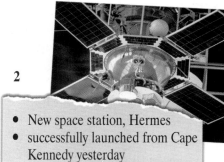

2
- New space station, Hermes
- successfully launched from Cape Kennedy yesterday
- remain in orbit around earth next eight months

7 Join the sentences below using the words in brackets.

1 Mrs Gingell gave birth to seven baby boys. They are all said to be doing well. (**who**)
2 An elephant was caught yesterday. It had escaped from Janneto's Circus. (**which**)
3 Doctor Tina White was awarded a prize. Her discovery will help save many lives. (**whose**)
4 The police have closed the road. The accident happened there. (**where**)
5 Ten people were injured yesterday. A bus overturned over in Westville. (**when**)

8 **a)** **Use words from the lists to fill in the blanks in the extracts below.**

damage, struck, homeless, casualties

1 An earthquake measuring 5.8 on the Richter scale **1)** .... the seaside town of Rexford early yesterday morning. No **2)** .... were reported but there was serious **3)** .... to the area and hundreds of people were left **4)** ....

alarm, broken into, witness, armed

2 The Westside Jewellery Shop on Main Street was **5)** .... late Sunday night. The burglars managed to get into the building without setting off the **6)** .... One **7)** .... said she saw two **8)** .... men running away from the shop carrying large bags.

survivors, cause, rescue workers, debris, trapped

3 **9)** .... yesterday freed the two remaining **10)** .... who were **11)** .... under **12)** .... from a collapsed warehouse on Friday. The **13)** .... of the accident is still unknown.

goals, celebrating, residents, championship, victory

4 **14)** .... of Brockton ran through the streets late last night **15)** .... Sussex United's **16)** .... over Leeds. Although Sussex were losing 2 - 0, they managed to score 3 **17)** .... in injury time to win the **18)** ....

b) **Which of the extracts above is about**

— an accident?   — a sports event?
— a natural disaster?   — a crime?

c) **Match the extracts to the following headlines.**

A ☐ **SURVIVORS SAFE AND SOUND**

B ☐ **FANS CELEBRATE SUSSEX'S TRIUMPH**

C ☐ *JEWELLERY SHOP BURGLED*

D ☐ **RESIDENTS SHAKEN AWAKE**

News reports, like narratives, describe events that happened in the past. However, the style is different. When writing a report you should:

- begin with a **summary** of the event
- include **accurate facts**
- use **formal** and **impersonal** style
- use **the passive**
- use **direct speech** to quote what people have said and **reported speech** to rephrase people's comments

When writing a story you should:

- begin by **setting the scene**
- use **chatty style**
- use **short forms**, **colloquial expressions**, variety of **adjectives/ adverbs**
- refer to the writer's/characters' **feelings**

9 **Match the beginnings to the endings, then answer the questions.**

BEGINNINGS...

1 ☐ Cyclist Neil Simms, aged 12, is recovering in hospital after being hit yesterday by a lorry belonging to Swifty Delivery.

2 ☐ It was a sunny afternoon and Neil Simms was cycling home from school. He was thinking about his plans for the weekend and he didn't see the delivery lorry which pulled out from a side road.

...ENDINGS

a Neil's dad smiled. "Thank goodness you're going to be alright," he said.

b Police announced that the driver would be charged with dangerous driving. Neil's father said that his son was lucky to be alive.

a Which beginning and ending is from a news report? Which is from a narrative?

b Do they describe the same event?

c Which extracts contain formal language?

d Which extracts contain colloquial language, adjectives and short forms?

10 **Read the sentences below and replace the words or phrases in bold with those given in the list.**

praised, furious, take action, comment on, presented with, denied all knowledge of, seriously injured, suffering from exhaustion, admitted responsibility for, refused to cooperate with

1 The Mayor of London was **badly hurt** in an accident on the motorway yesterday.

2 The young boy was **told he was good** for what he had done.

3 The factory owner refused to **say anything about** the story.

4 Local workers are **angry** about the plan.

5 He was eventually rescued from the cave when he was **feeling very tired**.

6 They are putting pressure on the government to **do something**.

7 Neither Suggs nor Dimkins **said they had caused** the accident.

8 Farnwell was **given** an award for his contribution.

9 Mrs Gaston **said she knew nothing about** the stolen painting.

10 The man who was arrested **said he would not help** the police.

11 **Rewrite the following sentences in the passive.**

1 A fire destroyed one of the museum's most valuable paintings.

....

2 We will give a prize to the writer of the best story.

....

3 A rescue team found the lost child in the mountains.

....

4 Heavy storms hit the east coast of the island late last night.

....

12 **Read the introduction and conclusion of the news report below and put the verbs in brackets into the correct active or passive tense. Then, use the pictures and prompts to write the main body of the report.**

BRUNTON BOMB MADE SAFE

A bomb left at Brunton train station **1)** .... **(make)** safe by explosives experts early this morning. The station **2)** .... **(close)** for two hours.

- bomb/hide/large shopping bag/left under bench/ platform 2
- it/report/by passenger/ at 7:00 am

- police immediately/ evacuated/station while/ explosives experts/ call
- nobody/hurt/in incident

No one knows who **3)** .... **(leave)** the bomb at the station and police do not know why Brunton **4)** .... **(choose)**. Detective George Browning said, "We **5)** .... **(want)** to speak to people who were in the area between 6:00 and 7:00 this morning. If you **6)** .... **(notice)** anything unusual, or if you saw anyone with a brown paper shopping bag, please call Brunton police station on 895 4117."

13 Rewrite the following sentences in reported speech, using verbs from the list.

promised, denied, informed, refused, announced, commented

1 "I give you my word that I will do everything in my power to help the victims of the earthquake," said the Mayor at the press conference.

....
....
....

2 The manager of the factory, Mr G Graham, said, "I will not say anything until I have all the facts."

....
....
....

3 When he was arrested, Mr Smith said, "I didn't take the money or the gold."

....
....
....

4 Doctor Godfrey told us, "The situation is serious but we are doing all we can."

....
....
....

5 Headmaster Mr P Brown said, "This is a great achievement for our students. I am proud of them all."

....
....
....

6 "The price of petrol will increase by 2p per litre from midnight on Tuesday," the Prime Minister said.

....
....
....

14 Last week a new music club opened in London. Read the advertisement and fill in the plan below. Then, use the completed plan to talk about the event.

OPENS FRIDAY, 20th June

SHAKE!
The BEST Music Club in the World!

No.1 pop singer ANY WONDER will open the club and perform live!

Don't Miss it!

5 Brunel Street, East London

SUMMARY OF EVENT
- Who: ....
- Where: ....
- When: ....
- What: *Shake!* music club opened

DETAILS
- 6pm: fans started queuing outside club
- 8.15pm: Any Wonder arrived — black limousine — signed autographs
- 9pm: Club opened doors
- 10pm: Any Wonder on stage

COMMENTS
- club owner Martin Lowe — "I hope the club will be a great success."

15 a) Read the rubric, underline the key words and answer the questions.

You are a reporter for *Music Echo* magazine and have been asked to write a news report about the opening of *Shake!* club. Write your **report**, giving a detailed description of the event and adding a suitable headline. (120-180 words)

1 What type of composition should you write?
2 Who is going to read it?
3 Should you include factual information?
4 Which of the following should you use? Tick (✓).
   everyday language ___ ; passive voice ___ ; formal linking words ___ ; variety of adjectives/adverbs ___ ; variety of reporting verbs ___ ; colloquial expressions ___ .

b) Use the notes in Ex. 14 to write your report about the opening of *Shake!* club. You can use the report in Ex. 3a) as a model.

UNIT 12b Reviews

1 **Look at the pictures and answer the questions:**

a) Would you rather read the book, or watch the film? Why?

b) What kind of book is it? What kind of film is it? Tick (✓)

	Book	Film
1 romance		
2 science fiction		

c) Can you think of any other types of books and films?

d) What's your favourite book/film?

e) What would you say to a friend to recommend a book or a film?

Reviews are short descriptions of books, films, plays, TV programmes, etc. They are written to inform readers and viewers, and to give them your opinion/recommendation about whether (or not) they should read a book or see a film/play/etc.

A review should consist of:

a) an **introduction** in which you summarise all the background information of the book/film/etc. (i.e. title, name of author/director, type, setting, etc);

b) a **main body** consisting of two paragraphs: one about the main points of the plot, presented in chronological order, and another including general comments on the plot, the main characters, the acting, the directing, etc.
 * **Note:** You should not reveal the end of the story to the reader.

c) a **conclusion** in which you recommend or do not recommend the book/film/play/etc, giving reasons to support your recommendation.

• Reviews are normally found in newspapers, magazines or as parts of a letter. The style you use depends on the publication and the intended reader and can be formal or semi-formal.

• You normally use **present tenses** and a variety of adjectives to describe the plot and make your comments more clear and to the point.

2 **Read the rubric and underline the key words, then answer the questions.**

The editor of the magazine you work for has asked you to write a review about a book you have recently read. Write your **review**, giving a brief summary of the plot and saying why you think other readers might enjoy it.

1 Who is going to read the review?

2 Which of the following must you include? Tick (✓).

A what type of book it is ☐

B the author's biography ☐

C the title of the book ☐

D how the story ends ☐

E the name of the author ☐

F main points of the plot ☐

G who the main characters are ☐

H how many of your friends have read it so far ☐

I whether or not you recommend it ☐

J general comments ☐

3 Which tenses would you use?

Introduction
· · · · · · · · · · · · ·
Paragraph 1

background information (title, name of author/ director, type, setting, etc.)

Main Body
· · · · · · · · · · · · ·
Paragraph 2

main points of the plot

Paragraph 3

general comments

Conclusion
· · · · · · · · · · · · ·
Paragraph 4

recommendation

3 a) **Read the book review and label each paragraph with the headings below.**

- *recommendation*
- *general comments*
- *main points of plot*
- *background information*

The Hound of the Baskervilles

Introduction

The Hound of Baskervilles, by Sir Arthur Conan Doyle, is an excellent <u>story that takes place in</u> London and Dartmoor. <u>This fascinating book is about</u> the famous detective, Sherlock Holmes, who with his trusted assistant, Watson, tries to solve the mysterious death of Sir Charles Baskerville.

Para 1
....
....

Main Body

<u>The mystery begins</u> when Dr. Mortimer, Sir Charles' personal doctor, relates the circumstances surrounding his patient's death to Holmes and Watson. The doctor believes that his death has something to do with the legend of the hound, which is an enormous, evil, hunting dog that terrorises the people of Baskerville. Soon, it becomes clear that Sir Henry, who is Sir Charles' nephew, and the only surviving heir to the Baskerville fortune, is also in danger. Holmes and Watson have to move quickly in order to protect Sir Henry's life and to solve the mystery.

Para 2
....
....

The book is full of thrilling moments as the author creates tension with unexpected twists and vivid descriptions. What gives the book its dark atmosphere, however, is the silent, evil presence of the legendary hound which dominates the story throughout.

Para 3
....
....

Conclusion

<u>I thoroughly recommend The Hound of the Baskervilles.</u> Readers will have a difficult time putting this masterpiece down as they are kept in suspense until the very end of the book.

Para 4
....
....

b) **Answer the questions.**

1 Which paragraph includes the writer's recommendation? What phrases does she use to recommend the book?
2 Which paragraph includes a short description of the main points of the plot? Does the writer reveal the end of the story?
3 In which paragraph does the writer include information about where the story takes place and what it is about?
4 Which paragraph includes general comments on the book? What are they?
5 Which of the following has the writer used? Tick (✓).
passive voice ___; variety of adjectives ___; colloquial expressions ___; abbreviations ___; complex sentences ___.

4 a) **Read the useful vocabulary box below. Which phrases refer to books? Which refer to films? Which refer to both?**

books *films*

USEFUL VOCABULARY

Background:
The film/book tells the story of ...
The film/story is set in ...
The book/novel was written by ...
The film is directed by ...
It is a comedy/horror film/love story.

Main points of the plot:
The story concerns/is about/begins ...
The plot is (rather) boring/thrilling.
The plot has an unexpected twist.

General Comments:
It is rather long/boring/confusing/slow.
The cast is excellent/awful/unconvincing.
The script is dull/exciting.
It is beautifully/poorly/badly written.
It has a tragic/dramatic end.

Recommendations:
Don't miss it. It is well worth seeing.
I wouldn't recommend it because ...
I highly/thoroughly recommend it.
It's bound to be a box-office hit.
Wait until it comes out on video.
It is a highly entertaining read.
It's a bore to read.

b) **Read the review in Ex. 3a again and replace the underlined sentences in the review with other appropriate ones.**

5 **Underline the correct word/phrase.**

1 The starring **role/character** is played by Jack Nicholson.
2 The **reader/audience** screamed when the murderer appeared.
3 *Angela's Ashes* is a well-**written/ acted** book that tells the struggle of a poor Irish family.

4 The plot has an unexpected **twist/cast** when little John finds out the truth.
5 The story has a **dull/tragic** end when the helicopter crashes on a mountain.
6 The **script/cast** of the film includes some of the hottest names in Hollywood.
7 The book is **based on/set in** the incredible life story of Charlie Chaplin.
8 *The Matrix* has the most spectacular **special effects/premieres** in film history.
9 *Mad Park* is a **box office hit/dull read**. You'll fall asleep after the second page.
10 *Captain Correlli's Mandolin* **plays the part/tells the story** of a young Italian soldier who falls in love with a Greek girl.

6 a) **Match the types of books/films to their definitions.**

Column A	Column B
1 comedy	A a film in which cartoons are brought to life
2 romance	B an exciting film full of adventure and danger
3 animated film	C a book or a film about a frightening story
4 mystery	D a film that makes people laugh
5 action film	E a book or a film about life in space/the future
6 science fiction	F the story of a person's life written by sb else
7 horror	G a book or a film about a love story
8 biography	H a book or a film about strange events that are not solved until the very end of the story

b) **Fill in the table below with adjectives from the list.**

dull, excellent, terrible, moving, superb, awful, fantastic, fascinating, touching, dreadful, thrilling, hilarious, entertaining, amusing

1	good/interesting	....
2	exciting	....
3	funny	....
4	sad	....
5	boring	....
6	bad	....

c) **Use adjectives from the table to talk about films/plays you have seen and books you have read, as in the example.**

e.g. *Dr Doolittle is one of the most amusing comedies I have ever seen.*

7 **Look at the chart and use words/phrases from the useful vocabulary box on p. 79 to write your recommendation for each book/film, as in the example.**

BOOKS *Readers' Poll*

1 *The English Patient*, by Michael Ondaatje
   Romance

2 *20,000 Leagues Under the Sea,* by Jules Verne
   Adventure

FILMS *Viewers' Poll*

3 *Sleep Well!* directed by Jack Miller
   Drama

4 *Stuart Little*, directed by Rob Minkoff
   Comedy

e.g. *I highly recommend The English Patient. It is a well-written and touching romance.*

RELATIVE CLAUSES

To make your review more interesting to the reader you can add details about the plot using *relative clauses*.

e.g. *Detective Larch wants to catch Scar. Scar is a diamond smuggler.*
→ *Detective Larch wants to catch Scar* **who is a diamond smuggler.**
William discovers a secret path. It leads to the castle.
→ *William discovers a secret path* **which leads to the castle.**
Claire is a teacher. Her son wins a scholarship to study biology.
→ *Claire is a teacher* **whose** *son wins a scholarship to study biology.*
They travel to York. In York they meet a very unusual taxi driver.
→ *They travel to York* **where they meet a very unusual taxi driver.**

8 Rewrite the extract using relative pronouns/adverbs. The words in bold show where you should add the relative clauses.

> The story is about a young woman named **Emily**. She is hired by a mysterious **lady**. Emily's assignment takes her to **Rio de Janeiro**. The man takes her on a dangerous **journey**.

1 She is a private detective.
2 The lady's uncle disappeared in Brazil.
3 In Rio de Janeiro, she meets a strange man called David Travis.
4 The dangerous journey eventually leads them into the heart of the Amazon Rainforest.

9 a) Read the rubric and underline the key words, then answer the questions.

A magazine has asked its readers to submit reviews of films that they have recently seen and think would be of interest to other people.

1 Who is going to read your review?
2 Which of the following must you include? Tick (✓).
　A ...... main points of the plot
　B ...... number of seats in the cinema
　C ...... type of film, name of director
　D ...... recommendation
　E ...... main characters and names of actors who portray them
　F ...... general comments about acting, soundtrack, etc

b) Read the film review. What is each paragraph about? How does the writer recommend the film? If you were to recommend this film, how would you recommend it?

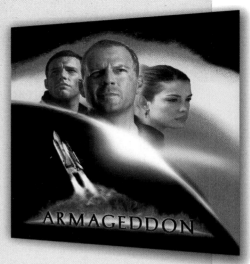

ARMAGEDDON

Introduction

1 Armageddon is an action packed adventure about an enormous asteroid and the desperate efforts of mankind to stop it from destroying the world. Directed by Jerry Bruckheimer, the cast includes Bruce Willis as Harry Stamper, an oil rig owner, Liv Tyler as his daughter, Grace, and Ben Affleck as Stamper's employee, A.J., who is in love with Grace.

Main Body

2 The story begins when NASA discovers that the gigantic asteroid is only eighteen days away from destroying the Earth. NASA asks Harry to prevent the deadly asteroid from reaching our planet. Harry and his oil rig crew are given intensive training by NASA astronauts before they travel to space.

3 The film is filled with suspense as the men race against time to save the planet. The special effects and computer graphics are so spectacular that the audience will be amazed. The actors give a brilliant performance and the directing is superb. What is more, the soundtrack, mostly by Aerosmith, is fantastic.

Conclusion

4 I thoroughly recommend this film. If you like excitement, it will definitely keep you on the edge of your seat. Don't miss it!

10 a) Read the rubric, underline the key words, then answer the questions.

Your teacher has asked you to write a film review for the school magazine. Write your **review** for the magazine, mentioning the main points of the plot, general comments about the acting, the directing, the plot, etc, as well as your recommendation(120-180 words).

1 Who is going to read your review? What tenses should you use?
2 Which of the following should you use? Tick (✓).
passive voice ___; variety of adjectives ___; colloquial language ___; complex sentences ___; abbreviations ___;
3 a) What type of film is it?　b) Who directed it?　c) Who stars in it? d) What characters do they play? e) What is the film about?
4 What are the main points of the plot? What general comments would you make? How would you recommend the film?

b) Use your answers in Ex. 10a to write your film review. You can use the review in Ex. 9 as a model.

UNIT 13 "For and Against" Essays

1 **a)** Look at the pictures and talk about the pros and cons of eating out at restaurants. Think about the service, the menu, the prices, and the atmosphere.

b) Read the points below, then listen to the cassette and tick those mentioned. Which of these points are advantages and which are disadvantages?

A	fun to eat out	☐	**D** expensive	☐
B	not as tiring as cooking	☐	**E** unhealthy	☐
C	have to book in advance	☐	**F** not hygienic	☐

"For and against" essays are one type of discursive writing in which you discuss the advantages and disadvantages of a specific topic. A "For and against" essay should consist of:

a) an **introduction** in which you present the topic, making a general remark about it <u>without</u> giving your opinion;

b) a **main body** in which you present the points for and the points against, in separate paragraphs, supporting your arguments with justifications/examples;

c) a **conclusion** which includes your opinion (e.g. *In my opinion/view, I believe/ think*, etc) or a balanced summary of the topic.

- You must <u>not</u> include opinion words (I believe, I think, etc) in the introduction or the main body. Opinion words can only be used in the final paragraph, where you may state your opinion on the topic.
- "For and against" essays are normally written in a **formal style**; therefore you should avoid using strong language (I know, I am sure, etc), short sentences, colloquial expressions or idioms.

You can find this type of writing in articles in newspapers, magazines, etc.

2 Read the rubric and underline the key words, then answer the questions.

> You have had a class discussion about different forms of travel. Your teacher has now asked you to write an **essay** presenting the arguments for and against travelling by boat.

1 What type of essay should you write?

2 Should you use short sentences, colloquial expressions and idioms? If not, why?

3 Which of the following points could be included in your essay? Tick (✓). Which points are pros and which are cons? Can you add any other ideas?

1	cheaper than other forms of travel	☐	4	journeys can take a long time	☐
2	can be unpleasant in bad weather	☐	5	more comfortable and enjoyable than other forms of transport	☐
3	lots of people go on sailing holidays	☐	6	famous explorers travelled the seven seas	☐

Introduction
. . . .
Paragraph 1

present topic (without stating your opinion)

Main Body
. . . .
Paragraph 2

arguments for, with justifications/examples

Paragraph 3

arguments against, with justifications/examples

Conclusion
. . . .
Final Paragraph

your opinion/balanced summary

3 a) **Read the article and label the paragraphs with the correct headings. What is the writer's opinion on the topic? Finally, replace the topic sentences in the main body paragraphs with alternative ones.**

- *arguments against*
- *arguments for*
- *opinion*
- *present topic*

Introduction

Did you know the boat was one of the first forms of transport? A hundred years ago, the only way to make a journey across the sea was by boat. Nowadays, however, when it is possible to fly from one continent to another in the space of a few hours, is there any reason to travel by boat?

Para 1
....
....
....

Main Body

Although the boat is a rather old-fashioned way of travelling, it has certain advantages. **To begin with**, boats are usually more comfortable than planes or cars. Instead of staying in your seat for the whole journey, you can go for a walk on the deck, eat in a restaurant, or even go shopping. Having more space to move around makes a long journey much more pleasant. **Furthermore**, boats are often cheaper than other forms of travel. **For example**, a boat ticket usually costs less than a plane ticket. **Finally**, boats are a safe alternative to cars and planes. There are fewer accidents at sea than in the air or on the roads.

Para 2
....
....
....

However, travelling by boat does have its disadvantages. It usually takes much longer than other forms of travel. **As a result**, it can be more tiring. **In addition**, boat trips can be very unpleasant when the weather is bad or the sea is rough, making journeys uncomfortable or even frightening.

Para 3
....
....
....

Conclusion

All things considered, although there are some disadvantages to travelling by boat, I believe it is a very enjoyable experience. Journeys may take longer, but if you have time to spare, you can take advantage of the many facilities which boats have to offer and enjoy a pleasant voyage.

Para 4
....
....
....

Useful expressions and linking words/phrases

- **to list and add points**: In the first place, To start/begin with, Secondly, Thirdly, Finally, In addition (to this), Furthermore, Moreover, Besides, etc.
- **to introduce or list advantages**: The main/first/most important advantage of..., One/Another/An additional advantage of..., One point of view in favour of..., It is often suggested/believed/argued that..., Some/Many people suggest/feel argue that..., Some/Many people are in favour of /are convinced that... etc.
- **to introduce or list disadvantages**: The main/most important disadvantage/drawback of..., One/Another/An additional disadvantage of..., One point/argument against..., Some/Many people are against... , etc.
- **to introduce examples/reasons/results**: for example/instance, such as, like, in particular, therefore, for this reason, because, as, since, as a result, etc.
- **to show contrast**: On the other hand, However, still, but, Nonetheless, Nevertheless, Although, Even though, Despite/In spite of (the fact that), etc.
- **to introduce a conclusion**: In conclusion, To conclude/sum up, All in all, Finally, Lastly, All things considered, Taking everything into account/consideration, etc.

b) **Read the article again and fill in the blanks below. Then, using expressions from the box on the right, talk about the pros and cons of travelling by boat.**

Main Body		Arguments	Justifications/Examples
	FOR		
Para 2		1) more comfortable than other forms of travel	go for a walk, eat in a restaurant, go shopping, have more space to move around
		2)	....
		3)	....
	AGAINST	Arguments	Justifications/Examples
Para 3		1)	....
		2)	....

4 Read the article again and replace the linking words/phrases in bold with synonymous ones from the table on p. 83. Then, say which of the linking words/phrases in the article are used to:

a) list/add points c) show contrast
b) introduce reasons/results d) introduce a conclusion

5 Underline the correct linking word/phrase.

1 **Besides/Despite,** television affects the way we think.
2 Many people **are against/argue that** we need advertisements in order to keep up to date with the latest products on the market.
3 One point of view **against/in favour of** travelling is that it allows you to meet people from different cultures.
4 **Even though/Nevertheless** most people nowadays use a computer at work, it will be a while before we stop putting our ideas down on paper.
5 **For instance/Still**, people who know how to play a musical instrument are usually popular and make friends more easily than others.

6 Read the paragraph below and underline the correct linking word/ phrase.

There are many advantages to having children at an early age. **1) To begin with/In addition to this**, when you are young, you have a lot of energy. This means you can cope quite easily with children's demands for constant care and attention. **2) To conclude/Secondly**, young parents can relate to their children and **3) therefore/nevertheless** understand them better. **4) Yet/Finally**, when you become a parent at an early age, you are still young enough to enjoy life when your child becomes independent.

MAIN BODY PARAGRAPHS

You should start each main body paragraph with a **topic sentence** which introduces or summarises the main topic of the paragraph. The topic sentence should be followed by supporting sentences which justify the argument presented in the topic sentence, by giving examples or reasons. You should use linking words/phrases to present your justifications, such as: *first of all, what is more, for example, because, since, in particular*, etc.

e.g. *Travelling by train has a lot of advantages.* } topic sentence

First of all, it is comfortable as trains are spacious so there is plenty of room to walk about. What is more, trains are convenient. For example, you do not have to take any food or beverages with you, because most trains have a restaurant. Finally, when you travel by train you reach your destination fairly quickly. } supporting sentences

7 a) Read the extract below and choose the correct topic sentence to fill in the blank.

1 There are many advantages to using the Internet.
2 However, there are many arguments against using the Internet.
3 Computers have become the most important means of communication.

....
....

First of all, you spend hours and hours sitting in front of a computer screen. This can lead to severe backache and problems with your eyesight. Moreover, using the Internet can be very expensive, because the membership fees and phone bills are often high. Finally, using the Internet requires a lot of patience. Getting onto the Internet is not always easy and this means you sometimes have to wait a long time to get access.

b) What is the topic of the paragraph? List the arguments mentioned.

8   **a)** Match each argument about modelling to its corresponding justification. Which points are "for" and which are "against"?

Arguments

1 [   ] be an exciting career
2 [   ] opportunity to earn a lot of money
3 [   ] models must constantly watch what they eat
4 [   ] no privacy

Justifications

a expected to stay thin so that they look good all the time

b designers and fashion magazines are willing to pay high fees for popular models

c reporters are always chasing them

d models usually travel to interesting places and often meet famous people

b) Use linking words/phrases to complete the main body paragraphs below.

e.g.   There are certain arguments in favour of a career in modelling.

....
....
....
....

On the other hand, many people believe that a career in modelling also has drawbacks.

....
....
....
....
....

TECHNIQUES TO BEGIN OR END YOUR ESSAY

To attract the reader's interest and make the beginning or ending of your essay more effective, you can use some of the following writing techniques:

a) **address the reader directly** e.g. *If you take the time to train your dog, it will learn to obey you.*

b) include **a quotation** (i.e. a sentence or phrase taken from a book, play, etc.) When we use a quotation, it is necessary to mention the name of the person who said/wrote it. e.g. *As George Orwell wrote, "All animals are equal, but some are more equal than others."*

c) include **a rhetorical question** e.g. *Is it true that a dog is man's best friend?*

9 Read the extracts below and say which are beginnings and which are endings. Then identify which writing technique(s) has/have been used in each.

A Do you fancy yourself as a handyman or handywoman? For people who are good with their hands, home decorating is certainly an option. With the wide range of materials available in the shops, and the increasingly high cost of professional decorating, the trend is towards DIY. So what are the advantages and disadvantages of 'do it yourself'?

B To sum up, although there are many points against being a reporter, I believe there are certainly aspects in favour of it. Besides, as John Hersey once said, "Journalism allows its readers to witness history."

C More and more couples today choose to have only one child. Most of us imagine that being an only child must be terribly lonely, but is that really the case? Having no brothers or sisters has both advantages and disadvantages.

D All things considered, I believe that there are more disadvantages than advantages to dieting. Perhaps that was why writer and journalist Geoffrey Cannon believed that "Dieting makes you fat." After all, if you eat sensible, well-balanced meals and keep fit and active, you are more likely to stay slim.

10 a) **Read the topic sentences and think of appropriate supporting ones. The prompts below will help you.**

1 There are certain drawbacks to being a doctor.
   - have to study all their lives in order to keep up with the latest medical developments
   - ....
     ....
   - ....
     ....

2 Watching television has certainly got its advantages.
   - keep up to date with current news
   - ....
     ....
   - ....
     ....

3 There are many arguments against being a famous rock star.
   - never home because they travel all over the world giving concerts
   - ....
     ....
   - ....
     ....

b) **Match the quotations to the topics above. Use the quotations to write appropriate endings for each topic.**

a ☐ "Everybody wants to be famous until they are."
Keith Richards (musician, songwriter)

b ☐ "We are humble men in our profession. We do our best."
A Dickson Wright (British surgeon)

c ☐ "Television! The entertainment which flows like tap water."
Dennis Potter (British playwright)

11 **Read the topic sentences, then write appropriate supporting ones. Join the sentences with appropriate linking words/ phrases in order to write a complete paragraph.**

1 There is no doubt that going on holiday during the winter is an attractive option.
....
....
....
....

2 On the other hand, there are drawbacks to being a firefighter.
....
....
....
....

3 There are certain disadvantages to owning a dog.
....
....
....
....

12 a) **Discuss the following questions in pairs.**

- Do many people in your country use bicycles instead of cars?
- What are the advantages and disadvantages of using a bicycle?
- What are the differences between cycling in the city and in the country?
- Do you think more people should cycle to work instead of using other forms of transport? Why?

b) **Read the rubric and underline the key words, then answer the questions.**

A health and fitness magazine has asked its readers to write an article discussing the advantages and disadvantages of cycling as a form of transport. Write your **article** for the magazine.

1 What type of essay is this?

2 Which of the following *should not* be included in your introduction? Tick (✓).

A your opinion ☐

B general remarks ☐

C statement about the topic ☐

D a quotation ☐

3 In which part of the essay should you write about the advantages and the disadvantages of cycling?

4 In which paragraph can you include your opinion about cycling?

c) **Look at the list of points below and tick the six points that should be included in your article. Mark these as A (advantages) or D (disadvantages), as in the example.**

1	cycling is an inexpensive form of transport	✓	*A*
2	fumes from cars and lorries are bad for your health	☐	☐
3	there are lots of different bicycles in the shops	☐	☐
4	cycling helps you to stay fit	☐	☐
5	cycling on busy roads is not very safe	☐	☐
6	my cousins go cycling at weekends	☐	☐
7	cycling is an environmentally-friendly way to travel	☐	☐
8	bicycles are unsuitable for long journeys	☐	☐

d) **Match the relevant points from above to the justifications below. Then, make sentences using appropriate linking words/phrases.**

A it is a good form of exercise, particularly for the legs, heart and lungs
B it does not create air pollution
C you do not have to spend money on things such as petrol or costly repairs
D drivers do not always give way to cyclists
E there is a limit to the distance a cyclist can reasonably travel in one day
F in some cities the fumes are so bad that cyclists have to wear masks to protect them from pollution

13 Use your answers from Ex. 12 to write your article on the advantages and disadvantages of cycling as a means of transport (120 – 180 words). You can use the text in Ex. 3a as a model.

1 Listen to a discussion about free healthcare and match the viewpoints with the reasons. Then, say which points you agree with and which ones you disagree with.

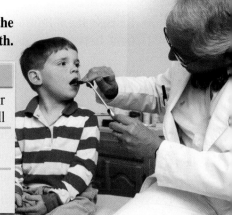

Viewpoints	Reasons
A free healthcare is a basic human right ☐	**1** people would learn to have healthier lifestyles, so fewer people would be ill
B people who can afford it should pay for their treatment ☐	**2** everyone deserves free medical treatment when they are ill
C more time and money should be spent on health education ☐	**3** more money could be spent on treating those who really need it

Opinion essays are discursive essays in which you present your personal opinion on a particular topic. Your opinion must be stated clearly and supported by justifications. You should also present the opposing viewpoint(s) in a separate paragraph.

An opinion essay should consist of:

a) an **introduction**, in which you introduce the subject and state your opinion clearly;

b) a **main body**, consisting of two or more paragraphs (each presenting a separate viewpoint supported by reasons/examples), including a paragraph giving the opposing viewpoint supported by reasons/examples; and

c) a **conclusion**, in which you restate your opinion using different words.

- You normally use **present tenses** in this type of writing, and phrases such as *I believe*, *In my opinion*, *I think*, *It seems to me that*, *I strongly disagree with*, etc to express your opinion. You should list your viewpoints with *Firstly, Furthermore, Moreover, Also*, etc, and introduce the opposing viewpoint using *However, On the other hand*, etc.

- Opinion essays are normally written in a **formal style**, therefore you should avoid using colloquial expressions, short forms or personal examples. You can find this type of writing in the form of an article in newspapers, magazines, etc.

2 Read the rubric and underline the key words, then answer the questions.

You have had a class discussion about the following statement:
   English and Maths are more important subjects than Art and Music.
Now your teacher has asked you to write an **essay** giving your opinion and reasons to support your view(s).

1 Who is going to read your essay?

2 Should you use colloquial expressions and short forms? Why (not)?

3 What does the statement in the rubric mean? Tick (✓)

  A Art and Music are easier than English and Maths. ☐

  B Art and Music are not as important as English and Maths. ☐

4 Which of the following should you include in your essay? Tick (✓).

  A reasons why Art and Music can be boring ☐

  B your views about whether English and Maths are important ☐

  C reasons or examples to support your views ☐

  D opposing views and supporting arguments ☐

Introduction
....

Paragraph 1

introduce the subject and state your opinion clearly

Main Body
....

Paragraph 2

first viewpoint and reasons/examples

Paragraph 3*

second viewpoint and reasons/examples

Paragraph 4*

opposing viewpoint and reasons/examples

Conclusion
....

Final Paragraph

restate your opinion, using different words

* *The number of paragraphs in the main body depends on the number of viewpoints included.*

5 Which of the four subjects mentioned in the rubric do/did you study at school? Which is/was your favourite, and why?

6 What are the benefits of studying these subjects? Use the notes to complete the table. You can add further ideas of your own.

tools to deal with everyday matters   *provide well-rounded education*
help you communicate clearly   *necessary in order to find a job*

English & Maths	Art & Music
....	....
....	....
....	....

7 Do you agree or disagree with the statement in the rubric? Give reasons.

3 a) **Read the essay and label the paragraphs with the headings below.**

- second viewpoint & examples
- restate opinion
- first viewpoint & examples
- subject & opinion
- opposing viewpoint(s)

English and Maths are more important subjects than Art and Music

Introduction

Isn't it unfortunate that in today's society there are so many people who cannot read, write or even do arithmetic? I strongly believe that, although subjects such as Art and Music are important, English and Maths are the most fundamental part of our education.

Para 1
....
....

Main Body

In the first place, when you know how to read, write and do simple calculations, you have the tools required in order to deal with everyday matters. For example, being able to read and write can help you communicate and express yourself clearly. Moreover, you need basic maths for such daily chores as doing your shopping, paying your bills and managing your money.

Para 2
....
....

Furthermore, it is essential to have a good knowledge of English and Maths in order to find even the simplest job. Reading, writing and mathematical skills are the minimum requirements that most employers demand.

Para 3
....
....

On the other hand, it can be argued that Art and Music are just as significant as English and Maths. For instance, learning how to draw or play an instrument can introduce a child to a whole new world. In addition to this, subjects such as Art and Music can provide children with a well-rounded education rather than just basic skills.

Para 4
....
....

Conclusion

All things considered, though, it seems to me that English and Maths are vital subjects. Without learning to read, write or do arithmetic, people may have difficulties coping with even the simplest tasks in daily life.

Para 5
....
....

b) **Read the essay again and underline the viewpoints the writer mentions. What reasons/examples are given to support each viewpoint? What linking words/ phrases are used to introduce the writer's viewpoints and the opposing viewpoint? What is the writer's opinion? Do you agree or disagree with this opinion?**

4 Use the linking words/phrases from the list below to fill in the table that follows, as in the example.

in the first place, also, for example, to sum up, moreover, firstly, although, to begin with, all things considered, such as, therefore, on the other hand, however, apart from this, in other words, in particular, for instance, in addition, because, taking everything into account, furthermore, for one thing, since, lastly, secondly, nonetheless, while

1	To list points:	*in the first place,* ....
2	To add more points:	....
3	To introduce opposing viewpoints:	....
4	To introduce examples/reasons:	....
5	To conclude:	....

5 Read the extracts and replace the linking words/phrases with suitable ones from Ex. 4. Which paragraph is each extract from?

A 1) On the other hand, computers save us time and energy and make our daily lives easier. **2) For one thing**, most of us are grateful to be able to withdraw money from cash machines rather than wait in long queues inside the bank. **3) What is more**, computers have made many people's jobs easier by doing routine tasks that in the past were tiring and time-consuming.

B 1) All in all, I don't believe that theatre is an outdated form of entertainment, **2) since** new ideas are often presented on the stage. **3) While** television may be more convenient, it is theatre that offers quality entertainment.

6 Underline the correct word/ phrase, as in the example.

1 **It is argued/One reason** that testing new drugs on animals is necessary before giving them to humans.

2 In my view, we can all do something to protect the environment. **For example/In addition**, we can recycle newspapers and magazines.

3 Taking holidays abroad is usually no more expensive than taking them in your own country. **What is more/However**, it gives you the opportunity to experience other cultures.

4 **Secondly/Especially**, regular exercise helps you to stay in good health.

5 On the other hand, it can be argued that what individuals do to protect the environment makes very little difference, **in particular/since** it is factories and power stations which create the most pollution.

Each main body paragraph should start with a **topic sentence** which clearly states the main idea of the paragraph. This should be followed by appropriate **supporting sentences** which justify the main idea and/or give examples.

7 Read the extract below and answer the following questions.

On the other hand, there are certain disadvantages to having your own car. Firstly, cars have to be maintained and repaired on a regular basis. Therefore, you need to spend a considerable amount of money to keep the car in good condition. Moreover, driving can sometimes be extremely stressful. For example, being caught in a traffic jam is not only irritating but also time-consuming.

a) What is the main idea of the paragraph? Which sentence is it in?

b) What supporting sentences does the writer give?

c) Which linking words/phrases has the writer used? Suggest other suitable words/phrases which could replace these.

8 Read the topic sentences and suggest suitable supporting ones.

1 Television may have a harmful effect on young people.

   ....

   ....

2 Looking after a pet from an early age develops a person's character.

   ....

   ....

3 Life in a large city is very interesting.

   ....

   ....

Useful expressions for giving opinions

- I believe/think/feel (that) ...
  I strongly believe ...
- In my opinion/view, ...
- The way I see it, ...
- It seems/appears to me (that) ...
- To my mind, ...
- I (do not) agree that/with ...

- My opinion is that ...
- As far as I am concerned, ...
- I (completely) agree that/with ...
  I (strongly) disagree that/with ...
- I am totally against ...
- I couldn't agree more that/with ...
  I couldn't disagree more that/with ...

9 Use the prompts below to write sentences, as in the example.

1 we / help / elderly ➡ their lives be easier
   e.g I strongly believe that we should help the elderly. If we were to do this, then their lives would be easier.

2 all students / learn / foreign language ➡ have better career opportunities

   ....

3 people / give up smoking ➡ have fewer health problems

   ....

4 teenagers / get / part-time job ➡ learn to be more responsible

   ....

5 we / all do / voluntary work ➡ our community be a better place to live

   ....

   ....

10 Use appropriate expressions to expand the prompts below to make sentences expressing an opinion, as in the example.

1 in order to / protect / environment / people / stop use / plastic bags
   It seems to me that, in order to protect the environment, people should stop using plastic bags.

2 spending money / set up / space stations / be / completely / unjustified

   ....

3 in order to reduce / pollution / traffic / be / ban from / enter / city centre

   ....

4 organic vegetables / be / much / healthy / than / vegetables / grown with chemical fertilizers

   ....

5 children / be encouraged / participate in / after-school activities

   ....

   ....

11 a) **Read the sentences below. Then, use appropriate words/ expressions to give your opinion, as in the example.**

1 A part-time job is the best option for someone who is a working parent.
I completely agree that a part-time job is the best option for someone who is a working parent.

2 Package holidays are ideal for people who do not like to travel alone.
....
....
....

3 Becoming more aware of environmental concerns is the only way to help save our planet.
....
....
....
....

4 Educational standards in private schools are usually higher than those in state schools.
....
....
....
....

5 Boxing is an extremely violent sport and should be banned.
....
....
....

12 a) **Imagine you have had a class discussion about the following question:** *"Should more people give up meat and become vegetarians?"* **Read the viewpoints (1-5) and match them to the reasons (A-E), as in the example.**

1 Eating meat is bad for you [B]

2 There are many healthy and tasty alternatives available ☐

3 Eating meat is cruel to animals ☐

4 Meat is an essential part of our diet; we cannot do without it ☐

5 Vegetarian food is often boring and tasteless ☐

A Soya beans and lentils are delicious and are good sources of protein.

D Animals are kept in terrible conditions just so they can be killed and eaten.

B It has been linked to heart disease and even cancer.

E There aren't many vegetarian dishes that actually taste nice.

C Meat provides us with the protein and vitamins that we need.

b) **Read the viewpoints again and say which you agree with and which you disagree with. Make sentences using appropriate linking words/phrases.**

c) **Complete the parts of the essay below, using your answers from parts a) and b) as well as your own ideas.**

Nowadays, we are often told what we should or should not eat. However, I personally believe ....
....

To begin with, ...
....

In addition, ...
....

On the other hand, ...
....

13 Read the extracts below and say which are beginnings and which are endings. Which writing techniques have been used in each?

    A addressing the reader directly
    B asking a rhetorical question
    C using direct speech/a quotation

1 Every day we hear of more and more violence at sports events because fans become enraged when their team loses. Don't you think that the most effective way to control such incidents would be to teach people how to handle defeat?

2 To sum up, competition has a negative effect on children, as the only thing that really matters is winning. Imagine how you would feel if you were always expected to be the best.

3 In conclusion, I strongly believe that taking part in sports is more important than victory itself. After all, as our coach always says, winning is just "the icing on the cake."

4 Has the importance placed on winning increased in recent years? For many people, this seems to be the main aim of sport. However, I believe that simply taking part is far more important than winning.

14 Read the rubric and underline the key words, then answer the questions.

> You have had a class discussion about the following statement:
> *Fast food is a good alternative to cooking for yourself.*
> Now your teacher has asked you to write an **essay** expressing your opinion and giving reasons for your point of view.

1 What does the statement in the rubric mean?
    A Fast food is cheap, delicious and good for you.
    B Fast food is a good solution for those who have no time to cook.
    C Cooking is easier than ordering takeaway.

2 Which points *must* you include in the essay?
    A your opinion   **B** your friend's opinion
    C reasons to justify your points of view

3 Which style is *not* suitable for this essay — formal or informal?

15 a) Read the rubric in Ex. 14 again and match the viewpoints (A - C) to their reasons/examples (1 - 6). There are two justifications for each viewpoint.

Viewpoints		
A fast food easy solution for people with busy lives	☐	☐
B fast food unhealthy	☐	☐
C fast food expensive for consumer and environment	☐	☐

Reasons / Examples
1 high in fat and salt; not fresh
2 packaging non-biodegradable, damages environment
3 many ingredients are genetically modified
4 ordering fast food saves time and energy
5 people who work long hours can pick up phone and order takeaway
6 money spent on fast food for a week is enough to buy groceries for two weeks

b) Which of the viewpoints agree with the statement in the rubric? Which disagree?

c) Use the notes in part a) to talk about fast food, as in the example.

e.g. *In the first place, fast food is very unhealthy. ...*

16 Read the rubric in Ex. 14 again, then write your essay (120 - 180 words). Use your answers from Ex. 14 and your notes from Ex. 15 to help you. You can use the essay in Ex. 3 as a model.

UNIT 14b Providing Solutions to Problems

1 Look at the pictures and answer the questions.

a) Which of the following is shown in each picture?
1) air pollution   ....
2) heavy traffic   ....
3) rubbish   ....

b) Do any of these problems exist in your town/city?

c) Can you think of any solutions to these problems?

Essays providing solutions to problems are pieces of writing in which you discuss a problem and its causes as well as the expected results or consequences of your suggestions. An essay providing solutions to problems should consist of:

a) an **introduction** in which you state the problem and/or what has caused it;

b) a **main body** which consists of two or more paragraphs presenting suggestions and their results/consequences. You should start a new paragraph for each suggestion and its results/consequences; and

c) a **conclusion** in which you summarise your opinion.

- Essays providing solutions to problems are normally written in a formal or semi-formal style, depending on who is going to read them and where they are published. They are usually found in newspapers and magazines.

2 Read the rubric and underline the key words, then answer the questions.

A local newspaper has asked its readers to write articles entitled *"How can we make our city a better place to live?"* Write your **article** suggesting ways to improve your city.

1 Who is going to read your article?

2 Look at the problems (1-5) and match them to the solutions (a-e). Which of these problems do you think is the most/least serious? Can you think of any more problems and solutions?

PROBLEMS	SOLUTIONS
1 ☐ air pollution	**a** provide more litter bins
2 ☐ heavy traffic	**b** move factories out of the city
3 ☐ nowhere for people to walk	**c** encourage people to use public transport
4 ☐ nowhere for children to play	**d** build more parks and playgrounds
5 ☐ litter	**e** build wider pavements

3 Match the solutions above to each of the results below. Then talk about the solutions and their results, as in the examples.

RESULTS

☐ 1 there would be fewer cars on the roads
☐ 2 the streets would be cleaner
☐ 3 the air would no longer be dangerous to breathe
☐ 4 children would have somewhere safe to play
☐ 5 people would be able to move around more easily

Introduction
....

Paragraph 1

state the problem(s) and/or the cause(s)

Main Body
....

Paragraphs 2-4*

suggestions and results/consequences

Conclusion
....

Final Paragraph

summarise your opinion

* The number of main body paragraphs depends on the number of suggestions you want to make.

e.g. *If people were encouraged to use public transport, there would be fewer cars on the roads.*
We should provide more litter bins. If we did this, the streets would be cleaner.

3 a) **Read the article and label each paragraph with the headings below.**

- *second suggestion & results/consequences*
- *summarise your opinion*
- *first suggestion & results/consequences*
- *state the problem*
- *third suggestion & results/consequences*

How can we make our city a better place to live?

by Jennifer Miller

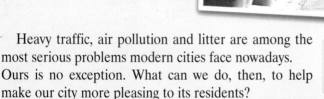

Introduction

Heavy traffic, air pollution and litter are among the most serious problems modern cities face nowadays. Ours is no exception. What can we do, then, to help make our city more pleasing to its residents?

Para 1
....
....

Main Body

First of all, it would be a good idea to encourage people to use public transport instead of their cars, especially when commuting to work. The result would be fewer cars on the roads, and therefore fewer traffic jams.

Para 2
....
....

Secondly, steps should be taken in order to solve the problem of air pollution. The situation could be improved if factories were moved out of the city. If this happened, the air would not be so polluted.

Para 3
....
....

Finally, efforts should be made to make our city a cleaner and healthier place to live. A useful suggestion would be to put more litter bins in the streets. If this was done, people would stop dropping their rubbish on the ground, and our city would be cleaner.

Para 4
....
....

Conclusion

There are many ways to make our city a better place to live. Adopting some of these measures would definitely result in better conditions for everyone.

Para 5
....
....

b) **Read the article again and answer the questions.**

1 What style has the writer used? Why? Give some examples.
2 What are the writer's suggestions and their results?
3 Which words/phrases has the writer used to introduce each of her suggestions?
4 Which writing technique has the writer used in her introduction? What other technique(s) could be used?

USEFUL VOCABULARY

To make suggestions:

- A useful suggestion would be to ...
- Another solution ...
- ... could be solved by ...
- Steps/Measures should be taken in order to solve/deal with ...
- Another way to ... is/would be to ...
- The situation could be improved if /by ...
- It would be a good idea if/to ...
- It would help if you/we/etc ...

To present results and consequences:

- This would ...
- Then ...
- By doing this, you/we/etc would ...
- If ... ..., the result would be ...
- The effect/consequence/result of ... would be ...
- In this way, ...

4 **Read the sentences and use the words/phrases in brackets to fill in the blanks, as in the example.**

1 More people should recycle paper. .... would be that fewer trees would have to be cut down. (**As a result, The result of this**)

2 According to many people, burglaries have increased recently .... that more and more people cannot find a job. (**due to the fact, because**)

3 If we used cars which run on lead-free petrol .... there would be less pollution. (**so that, it is certain that**)

4 TV programmes with violent scenes should be shown late at night .... children do not watch them. (**so that, in order to**)

5 Nuclear power plants should be closed down .... prevent the risk of an accident. (**so that, in order to**)

5 a) **Read the title below and then match the suggestions to their corresponding results.**

"How to **avoid stress** before **exams**"

Suggestions	Results
1 Take regular breaks.	A be healthy and able to concentrate
2 Study with a friend.	B work be more organised
3 Eat properly and get enough sleep.	C mind be clear and study time be more productive
4 Make a study plan.	D can discuss any difficulties that come up

b) **Using appropriate linking words/phrases write sentences, as in the example.**

*1 = C A useful suggestion would be to take regular breaks. **As a result**, your mind would be clear and your study time would be more productive.*

6 **Use topic sentences (A-D) to complete the paragraphs(1-4).**

A To begin with, retired people could join a social club.

B The problem of noise pollution could be solved by having cars and motorbikes checked on a regular basis.

C It would be a good idea for students to seek the advice of career counsellors.

D A useful suggestion would be to set up more national parks for endangered species.

1 ....

In this way, they would get professional advice and be less likely to make a wrong career decision. Also, students would become fully aware of all opportunities available in the labour market.

2 ....

It would also be a good idea for them to take up a hobby. By doing this, they would have the opportunity to meet people and also do something productive with their time.

3 ....

Another solution would be to introduce high fines for motorists whose vehicles cause excessive noise. As a result, the number of cars and motorbikes which disturb the peace would decrease.

4 ....
....

Animals living in a protected environment have a much better chance of survival. Moreover, national parks could provide programmes to help the animals breed.

7 Use the prompts below and appropriate linking words/phrases to write supporting sentences for the paragraphs that follow, as in the example.

> **A** • keep / outside of / house / well-lit / at night
> • install / alarm system
> • avoid / making / house / look / glamorous

To begin with we should make sure that our houses are not burglar friendly. *For example a useful suggestion would be to keep the outside of the house well-lit at night.* ....

> **B** • working out / three times / week / definitely / help / lose / weight / keep fit
> • follow / healthy diet / stop / eat / junk food

Secondly, it would be a good idea to join a gym. ....
....

> **C** • use / environmentally-friendly products / help reduce / water pollution
> • plant more trees / so that / there / be / more oxygen / fewer floods

Finally, steps should be taken to help save our planet. ....
....

> **D** • put up / signs / inform / public / if / they / litter / they / be fined
> • organise / clean-up days / once a week

A useful suggestion to keep our beaches clean would be to provide plenty of rubbish bins along them. ....
....
....

8 Read the rubric and underline the key words, then answer the questions.

> An educational magazine has asked its readers to submit articles discussing violence on TV and ways to stop this having negative effects on young people.

1 How many hours of TV do you watch every day? Do you watch violent programmes on TV? In what ways do you think they are harmful?

2 Which of the following suggestions would you make? Tick (✓).

A throw out your TV set ☐

B complain to your local TV station about unacceptable programmes and the hours they are shown ☐

C rent action-packed videos for your children to watch. ☐

D look at the TV guide and choose programmes which are suitable for children ☐

E put a TV set in their bedroom ☐

3 Now match the suggestions (A-E) to their results below.

☐ 1 ☐ your children would watch only educational and non-violent programmes

☐ 2 ☐ TV stations could be convinced to air certain programmes late at night.

4 In which paragraph should you state what the problem is? What useful vocabulary could you use to introduce suggestions? In which paragraph should you summarise your opinion?

9 Read the rubric in Ex. 8 again and write your article (120-180 words). Use your answers from Ex. 8 to help you. Use the article in Ex. 3a as a model.

UNIT 14c — Letters to the Editor

1 Look at the pictures and answer the questions.

a) What's the oldest/most beautiful building in your town/city?

b) How would you feel if it was torn down to have a modern block of offices built in its place?

c) If you wanted other residents to know what your views are, would you write: a narrative? a news report? a letter to the editor of a local newspaper?

Letters to the editor of a newspaper or magazine are written when you want to express your opinion about a topic that is of interest to the general public, to show your agreement or disagreement or to discuss a problem and suggest solutions.

Letters to the editor should consist of:

  a) an **introduction** in which you clearly give the reason for writing and your opinion about the topic;
     Note: If your letter is written in reply to another letter or article you should also mention where and when you read it, as well as the name of the person who wrote it.

  b) a **main body** in which you present the problems and their consequences or suggestions and results in separate paragraphs ;

  c) a **conclusion** in which you summarise your opinion or restate it using different words.

  • Letters to the editor are usually written in a formal or semi-formal style.

2 Read the rubric and underline the key words, then answer the questions.

> The local council of the town you live in has decided to build a large shopping centre. Write a **letter to the editor** of the local newspaper expressing your views on this matter.

1 Who is going to read your letter?

2 What is the reason for writing the letter?

3 How would you begin and end your letter? Why?

4 a) Is there a shopping centre in your town? What can you buy there? Is it popular with shoppers?

   b) Which of the following problems can a shopping centre cause? Tick (✓).
      noise pollution ☐   heavy traffic ☐   litter in the streets ☐   sea pollution ☐

   c) Would you like a new shopping centre near your house? What would be the advantages or disadvantages? Think about: crowded streets; convenience; noise/air pollution; variety of shops; traffic; smaller shops closing down; how the area will change; etc

Introduction

Paragraph 1

reason for writing and your opinion

Main Body

Paragraphs 2-3*

problems and consequences or suggestions and results

Conclusion

Final Paragraph

summarise/restate your opinion

* The number of main body paragraphs may vary depending on the rubric.

3 **a) Read the letter below and label the paragaphs with these headings:**

- *second problem and consequences*
- *reason for writing and opinion*
- *summary of opinion*
- *first problem and consequences*

Introduction

Dear Sir/Madam,

I am writing about Trent Council's decision to build a large shopping centre in our town. I strongly disagree with this decision and I believe it will have negative effects on the town.

Para 1
....
....

Main Body

Firstly, a shopping centre will turn Trent from a quiet, peaceful neighbourhood into a busy shopping area. Obviously, there will be an increase in the amount of traffic and the number of people coming into town. As a result, we will suffer from both air and noise pollution.

Para 2
....
....

Secondly, the appearance of our town will change completely. In order for the shopping centre to be built, some of our oldest and most beautiful buildings will have to be torn down. Therefore, Trent's surroundings as well as its character will be destroyed.

Para 3
....
....

Conclusion

To sum up, I am totally opposed to the Council's decision as I believe it will be disastrous for Trent. Consequently, I hope that the council will reconsider its decision.

Para 4
....
....

Yours faithfully,
Mary Swanson

b) Does the writer agree or disagree with the local council's decision?

4 **Read the letter again and complete the table that follows. Then make sentences, as in the example.**

		Problems	Consequences
Main Body	**Para 2**	• increase in amount of traffic and number of people ⟶	....
	Para 3	• .... ⟶	....

e.g. *The amount of traffic and number of people will increase. As a result, we will ...*

USEFUL EXPRESSIONS AND LINKING WORDS/PHRASES

- To begin your letter: I am writing to express my approval/disapproval of/support for ...; I am writing with regard to ...; I am writing about ...; I have just read a ... in your ... about ...; etc

- To state your opinion: In my opinion ...; I (do not) feel/believe/ think ...; I am (totally) opposed to/in favour of ...; I strongly agree/disagree with ...; etc

- To express consequences/results: This will/would mean ...; Then ...; Therefore ...; Consequently ...; As a result ...; If we do/did this ...; Obviously ...; Clearly ...; etc

- To list your points: Firstly ...; First of all ...; Secondly ...; Furthermore ...; What is more ...; Lastly ...; Finally ...; etc

- To end your letter: I hope my comments/suggestions/etc will be taken into consideration ...; I hope the government/local council/we will ...; I hope something will be done about this urgently, etc

5 **Read the letter in Ex. 3a again and underline the words/ phrases the writer has used which also appear in the table above. Then, replace those words/phrases with suitable alternatives, as in the example.**

e.g. *I am writing about = I am writing with regard to*
I strongly disagree with = I am opposed to

99

6 Use the prompts below to write full sentences, as in the examples.

1 opinion, / need / build / more schools.
In my opinion, we need to build more schools.

2 I / strongly believe / driving test / make / more difficult.
I strongly believe that the driving test should be made more difficult.

3 I / opposed / construction / new motorway

....

4 furthermore, / council / provide / more sports centres

....

5 I / write / express / disapproval / plans / close / The Majestic Cinema

....

6 I / feel / cars / ban / city centre

....

7 I / think / more policemen / patrol / our / neighbourhood

....

8 I / believe / new library / be / excellent idea

....

9 I / hope / comments / take / consideration

....

7 First match the beginnings with their endings and then answer the questions that follow.

BEGINNINGS...

1 I am writing in reply to a letter I read in your magazine. I strongly disagree with the views of the writer about cyclists. Being a cyclist myself, I know how thoughtless car drivers can be.

2 I am writing about the recycling plant to be built in our town. To my mind, it's high time we did something to help our environment.

...ENDINGS

A To sum up, I have to state that I am in total agreement with the council's decision to build the recycling plant.

B In conclusion, it is my opinion that motorists should be more considerate. After all, they are not the only ones on the roads.

a What is the reason for writing each letter?

b What is the writer's opinion in each case?

8 Read the suggestions below and match them to their results. Then, make sentences using appropriate linking words/ phrases and expressions, as in the example.

SUGGESTIONS
1 *C* companies have flexible working schedules
2 ☐ all shops open from 10 am to 9 pm during the week
3 ☐ pedestrians always use zebra crossings
4 ☐ all blocks of flats have security guards
5 ☐ airport built 20 km away from city centre
6 ☐ the newspaper have weekly supplement on cultural happenings in town

RESULTS
A avoid the risk of being hit by motorists
B tenants protected on a 24-hour basis
C employees be able to choose the hours that suit them
D residents will not be affected by air traffic
E people be better informed and have the opportunity to book tickets in advance
F working people will not be restricted as to when to do their shopping

e.g. *1 = C*
In my opinion all companies should have flexible working schedules. This would mean that employees would be able to choose the hours that suit them.

9 **a) Read the rubric and underline the key words, then answer the questions.**

> You saw the news report below in Monday's edition of the *Rosemary Telegraph* and have decided to write a **letter to the editor** making suggestions on how to make the park more appealing.

Late last night the local council finally decided in favour of making Rosemary Park more appealing to the city's residents. After a month of discussions, the council agreed to spend more than £50,000 on improving it. The council plans to complete work on the park by next June.

1 Who is going to read your letter?
2 What is your reason for writing the letter?
3 How would you begin and end your letter?

b) Match the facilities in column A to their functions in column B. Then, ask and answer questions, as in the example.

Column A	Column B
1 a snack bar	A bring your own food and have a picnic
2 drinking fountains	B wash your hands, change babies' nappies, etc
3 swings, sandboxes, etc	C have a drink whenever you are thirsty
4 picnic tables	D enjoy a cool drink and have something light to eat
5 public lavatories	E not drop rubbish on ground
6 litter bins	F children can play safely and have fun

1 = D A: Do you think the park should have a snack bar?
B: Yes, I do. Then we would be able to enjoy a cool drink and have something light to eat.

c) What else do you think a park should have?

10 **Read the rubric in Ex. 9 and the news report again and write your letter (120-180 words). Use your answers from Ex. 9 to help you. Use the letter in Ex. 3 as a model.**

1 You will hear a discussion about a health farm. Read the questionnaire below, then listen to the cassette and tick (✓) the correct boxes. Listen again to fill in the missing information. Finally, use the table to talk about the health farm.

	Excellent ☆☆☆☆	Good ☆☆☆	Average ☆☆	Poor ☆
Location	☐	☐	☐	☐
only an hour from .... , the nearest station twenty minutes away				
Facilities	☐	☐	☐	☐
.... courts, beautiful large bedrooms, a swimming				
Treatments	☐	☐	☐	☐
many on offer, ... choice, all wonderful				
Food	☐	☐	☐	☐
rather .... and tasteless, but low in fat and very				

General Comments
Oaklands' facilities very .... ; an excellent .... of treatments available; food rather .... — the menu could be improved

Reports are normally written for someone in authority (e.g. your employer, the local council, the head of a committee, etc) and contain factual information.

Assessment reports present and evaluate the positive and negative qualities of a person (i.e. an employee) or a building/place (i.e. a hotel, a restaurant, a shop, a cinema complex, etc) in order to make a judgement or recommendation about them.

Proposal reports present suggestions, plans or decisions about future actions.
Reports should consist of:
  a) an **introduction** in which you state the purpose and content of the report;
  b) a **main body** in which you present each topic in detail under suitable subheadings. (these headings introduce the topic of the paragraphs, so you do not need to start each paragraph with a topic sentence);
  c) a **conclusion** which summarises the information from the main body and states your general assessment and/or recommendation.
  • Reports are written in a formal, impersonal style. You should use factual language, passive voice and full verb forms. You should also write fairly short sentences to help your reader pick out the information easily. Present tenses are normally used for **assessment reports**. Past tenses can be used for reports related to past events. Modals, conditionals or would are normally used for **proposal reports**.
  • You should always begin your report by stating who the report is addressed to and what their position is, the writer's name and position, what the report is about and the date.

> e.g. **To:** Thomas Prescot, Chairman of Council
> **From:** Mary Scott, Senior Manager
> **Subject:** Big Screen Cinema Complex
> **Date:** 3rd June, 20...

Introduction

Paragraph 1:
state the purpose and content of your report

Main Body

Paragraphs 2-5*:
summarise each point under suitable subheadings
[**Assessment:** positive and negative points

Proposal:
suggestions/ recommendations]

Conclusion

Final Paragraph:
general assessment and/or recommendation

* The number of main body paragraphs may vary depending on the rubric.

2 Read the rubric and underline the key words, then answer the questions.

> You are an assistant manager for an international publishing company which is producing a tourist guide to restaurants in your country. The manager of your company has asked you to assess a restaurant in your area to see if it is suitable for tourists on a tight budget. Write your **report**, describing the restaurant's food, service, prices and atmosphere.

1 What is the aim of this report? What type of report should you write?

2 Who is going to read your report?

3 What is your position, according to the rubric?
   A manager of the company
   B assistant manager
   C reporter

4 What does "tourists on a tight budget" mean?

5 Which of the following *must* be included in the report? Tick (✓).
   A size of restaurant ☐
   B location of your town ☐
   C quality of food ☐
   D what the atmosphere is like ☐
   E what the service is like ☐
   F good and bad points of the restaurant ☐
   G location of restaurant ☐
   H high/low prices ☐
   I opening hours ☐

6 What style should you use? What are the main characteristics of this style?

7 Answer the following questions.
   a How often do you eat out? What is your favourite restaurant? How much do you usually spend when you eat out?

b Use the adjectives below to describe the food, the service, the prices and the atmosphere in a restaurant, as in the example.
   delicious, expensive, relaxing, disgusting, noisy, slow, reasonable, efficient
   e.g. *The food in ... is delicious.*

3 a) Read the report below and underline the correct word(s) in bold. Then, use the subheadings from the list to fill in the blanks.

   • *Food*   • *Atmosphere*   • *Recommendation*
   • *Service*   • *Prices*   • *Introduction*

To: Mr A J Williams,
         Manager,
         Burton Publishing
From: Milton Briggs,
         Assistant Manager
Subject: Gaslights Restaurant
Date: 21st July, 20....

Introduction

A) ....
The aim of this report is to assess the suitability of Gaslights Restaurant for tourists on a tight budget.

Main Body

B) ....
Gaslights serves good quality meals.
It has a wide variety of delicious local and international dishes **1) as well as/but** an excellent choice of starters and desserts. The menu **2) and/also** includes a number of French specialities.

C) ....
3) Nevertheless/Despite the fact that the staff at Gaslights Restaurant are well-trained and polite, the service can sometimes be slow. This can be a problem when the restaurant is full.

D) ....
The prices are quite reasonable. **4) Although/However**, some dishes, such as the French specialities, are rather expensive.

E) ....
Gaslights has a charming and relaxing atmosphere. The background music is pleasant **5) and/too** the soft lighting creates a cosy atmosphere. These elements, combined with the modern decor, appeal to customers of all ages.

Conclusion

F) ....
6) All in all/Even though the service can sometimes be slow, Gaslights offers first-class food at reasonable prices. **7) Therefore/ However**, I highly recommend this centrally-located restaurant for tourists on a tight budget.

b) Read the report again and fill in the table with the positive and negative points of Gaslights Restaurant. Then, use the information to talk about the restaurant.

Subheadings	Positive Points	Negative Points
Food	....	
Service	....	....
Prices	....	....
Atmosphere	....	

c) Would you recommend Gaslights Restaurant? Why(not)?

4 a) Join the sentences below using appropriate linking words/ phrases, as in the example.

however, in addition, therefore, as, on the other hand, and, although, alternatively

1 Annual membership fees at the Little Dale Sports Centre are quite reasonable. *However*, there are no special prices offered for students and young people.

2 To sum up, the local museum has interesting exhibits that will attract schoolchildren. It is ...., the most suitable choice for the school's day trip.

3 .... the function rooms of Hotel Royale are available for bookings throughout the year, they are often fully booked from November to January .... they cater for Christmas and New Year parties during this period.

4 The restaurant offers a wide choice of dishes at a range of prices. .... , buffets are available at very reasonable rates. .... , there are few vegetarian dishes.

5 The Italian Restaurant is located on the south bank of the river .... is easily accessible by underground. .... , for those who would rather use the bus, the number 397 from Central Square passes directly in front of the restaurant.

b) Choose five of the following subheadings below to match the extracts in part a).

A	2	Recommendation
B		Decor and Atmosphere
C		Location and Access
D		Fees
E		Facilities
F		Availability and Booking
G		Food

USEFUL EXPRESSIONS

You can start a report with the following phrases:
The purpose/aim of this report is to assess...
This report was carried out to assess...
As requested, this report is to assess ...

To end your report you can use the following phrases:
On the whole, .../To sum up, .../All in all, .../In conclusion, ...
In spite of the (dis)advantages, .../I would (not) recommend .../... is (not) recommended .../... is (not) suitable for ...

5 Read the rubric and underline the key words, then answer the questions.

You work for a company which is planning to hold its annual winter excursion. The manager has asked you to write a report about the suitability of the Mountain High Hotel for the excursion. Write your **report**, including information about rooms, facilities, food and cost, as well as commenting on the hotel's good and bad points.

1 What is the aim of this report? What type of report should you write?
2 Who is going to read your report?

6 a) Read the prompts below and match them to the correct subheadings.

- private bathroom in each room
- cosy lounge with fireplace
- breakfast not included in price
- £60 double room, £45 single room
- limited choice of dishes for vegetarians
- comfortable rooms with colour TV
- live music every weekend

- no special rates for groups with fewer than thirty people
- free skiing lessons
- three-star restaurant
- no telephones in rooms
- no room service
- delicious home-made meals
- guests can rent skiing equipment
- varied menu

Rooms: ....
Facilities: ....
Food: ....
Cost: ....

b) Which points are positive and which are negative?

c) Can you think of a suitable introduction?

d) What recommendation would you give?

7 Read the rubric in Ex. 5 again and write your report (120-180 words). Use your answers from Ex. 6 to help you. You can use the report in Ex. 3a) as a model.

8 Mark the statements below as T (for true) or F (for false).

In formal style we use:

1 long, sophisticated sentences ☐
2 factual language ☐
3 colloquial expressions ☐
4 formal linking words/phrases ☐
5 short forms ☐
6 advanced vocabulary ☐
7 formal idioms and phrasal verbs ☐
8 everyday vocabulary ☐
9 passive voice ☐
10 impersonal language ☐

9 The extracts below are written in a wrong style. Read them and replace the words/phrases in bold with more suitable ones from the lists.

finally, excellent, what is more, for example, fashionable, therefore

A Riverside Mall is one of the most convenient centres in our city. **1) What I mean is**, it is located near the main bus terminal and **2) so** it is easily accessible to shoppers. **3) Also**, there are many **4) trendy** restaurants where shoppers can eat lunch or dinner. **5) The last thing is**, there are **6) good** facilities for people with special needs.

increase the number of, the aim of this report is

B 1) I've written this report to recommend ways to **2) get more** foreign students at Silversmythe's College

to sum up, offered, special, attract

C 1) To cut a long story short *Photorama* would **2) bring in** more customers if **3) lower** prices were **4) given** to those studying photography.

10 Read the rubric and underline the key words, then answer the questions.

> You have a part-time job in a bookshop that specialises in educational publications. The manager wants to attract young customers to the bookshop and has asked you to write a **report** making your suggestions.

1 What is the aim of this report?

2 What type of report should you write: an assessment report or a proposal report?

3 Who is going to read your report?

4 What would make a bookshop popular with young people? Choose from the list below.

   A offer magazines and books of interest to young people — e.g. about fashion, computers, etc

   B not more than five people allowed in the shop at the same time

   C fun items on sale, such as posters and stickers

   D brighter decor

   E discounts for students

   F leaflets distributed to schools

5 What style should you use in your report? What are the characteristics of this style?

11 a) Read the report and choose appropriate subheadings from below to fill in the blanks.

- Location
- Purpose
- Service
- Conclusion
- Shop Interior
- Other Items on Sale
- Types of Books
- Discounts

To: Elizabeth Jones, Owner, Bookworms Bookshop
From: Sarah Thompson, Shop assistant
Subject: Attracting young customers
Date: 4th May, 20...

A) ....
The purpose of this report is to suggest ways to attract more young customers to the bookshop.

B) ....
Most of the books currently available are quite academic and therefore appeal to older customers. In order to encourage more young people to buy books, the shop should offer magazines and books on topics such as music, fashion and computers.

C) ....
At present the shop sells traditional stationery and calendars. It would be a good idea to stock items designed for young people, such as school equipment, posters, stickers, school bags and games.

D) ....
Discounts would encourage local students to buy their textbooks at the bookshop. In addition, leaflets should be given to schools and colleges to make students aware of these discounts.

E) ....
The inside of the shop is very plain and rather old-fashioned. Young people would be more likely to come in if the decor was modernised and the interior was painted in bright colours.

F) ....
In conclusion, the bookshop would attract younger customers if a wider range of goods were stocked, the interior was made more attractive and special prices were offered to students.

b) **Answer these questions.**

1 In which paragraph(s) does the writer mention her suggestions? What are these suggestions?

2 Underline the modals used in the report.

3 Can you think of another way to state the purpose of the report?

12 a) **Read the rubric and underline the key words, then answer the questions.**

> You have recently started working at a youth club. The manager wants to make the club more popular with 10- to 14-year-olds and has asked you to write a report making your suggestions. Write your **report** (120-180 words).

1 Who is going to read your report?
2 What is the purpose of the report?
3 What type of report should you write?
4 Should you use subheadings? What could they be?
5 In which paragraph(s) should you make your suggestions?

b) **Match the main points to the suggestions. Then, make sentences using appropriate linking words/phrases.**

Main Points
1 **A** interior of Thorntree Youth Club — not decorated in a way that appeals to younger children
2 ☐ youth club's current facilities more suitable for older teenagers
3 ☐ current publicity not aimed at younger children
4 ☐ youth club not open until 7 pm — rather late for 10- to 14-year-olds

Suggestions

A colourful posters put up — modern furniture bought — would brighten up the club premises

B club open earlier — younger children could go there straight from school

THORNTREE Youth Club
all children welcome
Tel: 0931-829913 for more information

C give out leaflets at schools — 10- to 14-year-olds would find out about the club

D organise activities — e.g. table tennis tournaments or computer games — more fun for 10- to 14-year-olds

c) **Choose suitable subheadings for the main body paragraphs of the report. Then, match them to the main points (1-4) in part a), as in the example.**

A Facilities	✓	2		**D** Decor		☐	☐
B Membership	☐	☐		**E** Publicity		☐	☐
C Opening Hours	☐	☐		**F** Location and Access		☐	☐

13 Read the rubric in Ex. 12 again and write your report (120-180 words). Use your answers from Ex. 12 to help you. You can use the report in Ex. 11 as a model.

Revision & Extension Section

INTERPRETING RUBRICS

Some rubrics do not fall neatly into a single writing type such as a description, a report, an opinion essay, etc. Instead they require a mixture of writing types.
e.g. *"... a letter describing a birthday party you attended ..."* - this is both a letter and a description of a celebration.
When you answer questions you should always remember to pay careful attention to key words, which show:

- **Type of writing -** words/phrases such as *"describe"*, *"give points for and against"*, *"assess"*, *"recommend"*, etc indicate the type of writing and layout expected.
- **Situation and intended reader -** key words/phrases such as *"you work for"*, *"your teacher has asked you"* etc indicate who you are writing to.
- **Subject -** key words/phrases indicate the main subject(s) of your piece of writing — e.g. *the environment, education, a festival, a famous person*, etc.
- **Topics to include -** most rubrics give you a list of the main topics to be included — e.g. *"... include a description of physical appearance, personal characteristics and lifestyle ..."*; this list provides you with the paragraph plan for the main body of your piece of writing *(e.g. paragraph 2 - physical appearance; paragraph 3 - personal characteristics; paragraph 4 - lifestyle).*
- **Other points to include -** phrases such as *"and explain why"*, *"then make suggestions about"* , *"say which you prefer"*, etc indicate important additional aspects that <u>must</u> be included in your piece of writing.

1 Read the rubric and underline the key words, then answer the questions.

> A close relative of yours got married last weekend. Your cousin, who lives in another city, was not able to come to the wedding. Write a **letter** to your cousin, describing the wedding. Describe the whole day, including preparations, the ceremony itself and some of the people who attended.

1 What type of composition is this?

2 **a)** Which of the following are you asked to describe? Tick (✓):

   A preparations in the weeks before the celebration ☐

   B preparations on the morning of the celebration ☐

   C some of the people who came ☐

   D some of the people who were unable to attend ☐

   E the wedding ceremony ☐

  b) In which part of the letter would you describe each topic? How many paragraphs would you need?

3 In which paragraph should you state your reason for writing?

4 Which of the following should your conclusion contain? Tick (✓):

   A details about the people who came ☐

   B closing remarks ☐

   C description of the activities in the evening ☐

2 Read the letter and label the paragraphs, then answer the questions.

- people who attended
- actual ceremony
- closing remarks
- preparations
- opening remarks & reason for writing

Introduction

Dear Iris,

I hope you're well. It's a pity you couldn't make it to Kim's wedding. We had a really wonderful time and I thought I'd write to tell you all about it.

Main Body

I went over to Kim's house at about 9am to help her get ready and do her make-up. When her bouquet arrived at the house, Kim cried because it looked so beautiful. The hairdresser did a lovely job with Kim's hair and we managed to get her ready in time.

Kim looked stunning as she walked down the aisle. Jim looked great in his dark blue suit, too. They were just the perfect match! The hymns were lovely and a soloist sang *Ave Maria*. It was very touching. After they had said their vows, they exchanged rings. Kim's mum didn't stop crying throughout the whole ceremony.

Do you remember Mrs Peacock, Kim's red-haired piano teacher? Well, she was there, wearing a funny hat — and you should have seen Uncle Bob! I've never seen him dressed so smartly. It certainly was a wedding to remember.

Conclusion

Anyway, Iris, I must go now. Take care, and I hope to see you soon.

Love,

Jess

Para 1
....
....
....

Para 2
....
....
....

Para 3
....
....
....

Para 4
....
....
....

Para 5
....
....
....

how/things with you?/sorry you/ not make it/Kim's wedding/ let me tell/ all about it

well that/ all for now/ give my love/ your mum/dad/ write soon/ tell me your news

Introduction ....

Paragraph 1

reason(s) for writing opening remarks

Main Body ....

Paragraph 2

preparations

Paragraph 3

description of the ceremony

Paragraph 4

brief description of some of the people at the celebration

Conclusion ....

Final Paragraph

closing remarks

1 Is this formal, semi-formal or informal letter?

2 What are the characteristics of this type of writing? Find examples in the letter of each characteristic.

3 What has been included in the introduction?

4 Which paragraph includes a description of the people who attended?

5 Underline the descriptive adjectives used in the letter, then replace them with suitable synonyms.

3 Read the introduction and conclusion again, then use the prompts given to write an alternative beginning and ending to the letter.

USEFUL LANGUAGE

- When you give your views on a topic, you can use linking words/phrases to **list points** — e.g. *To begin with, What is more, In addition,* etc
- The following linking words/phrases are useful to introduce **reasons** or **justifications** for your viewpoints — *This means that, As a result, so, because, Needless to say, therefore,* etc
- When you give examples to support your viewpoints, you can introduce these with the following linking words/phrases — *for example, for instance, such as,* etc
- You can use Type 0 and Type 1 conditionals to provide **examples** —
  e.g. *For instance, if you are worried or upset about something, spending time with your pet helps/can help you to forget your problems.*
- You can use Type 2 conditionals to introduce **suggestions** —
  e.g. *If I were a factory owner, I wouldn't pollute the environment.*
  If everyone took their rubbish home with them, our beaches wouldn't be so polluted.

4 Read the rubric, underline the key words and answer the questions.

> Your favourite magazine is holding a competition to find the best article with the title "The Perfect Pet". You should say what pet you would like to have, giving reasons. You should also mention how you would take care of your pet. The winning article will appear in the magazine. Write your **article** for the competition (120-180 words).

1 Who are you writing for?
  A the editor of a newspaper
  B the readers of a magazine
  C pet owners

2 Which topics *must* be included in your article? Tick (✓):
  A ☐ reasons why your article should be chosen
  B ☐ your ideal pet
  C ☐ suggestions about how to take care of the pet
  D ☐ reasons for your choice of pet
  E ☐ points for and against having a pet

3 In which order will you present the correct topics?

4 Look at the pictures and say which pet you would like to have, then give reasons for your choice. Use the prompts below and add your own ideas.

- make good companions
- make you feel happy
- loyal
- easy to look after

- obedient
- affectionate
- ....
- ....

5 What would your pet need? Choose from the list below and add ideas of your own.

- the correct food
- toys to play with
- regular exercise
- obedience training
- regular check-ups at the vet
- love and affection
- ....
- ....

5 Read the article and put the verbs into the correct conditional form. Then, answer the questions.

The Perfect Pet

1▶ We often hear people say that a dog is "man's best friend", which in my opinion is true. Many animals make good pets, but my ideal pet is a dog.

2▶ To start with, dogs make perfect pets because they are good companions. A dog keeps you company and understands your moods. For example, if you **1)** .... **(be)** sad, a dog comforts you and **2)** .... **(cheer)** you up. If you are happy, then a dog **3)** .... **(respond)** with playfulness.

3▶ In addition, dogs make the most loyal pets because they feel great affection for their owners and like to please them. If you train your dog, it **4)** .... **(become)** very obedient because it **5)** .... **(learn)** to behave in the way you want it to.

4▶ What is more, dogs can be very useful. For instance, they are often used to guard property, or to guide blind people. Even dogs who are just pets have been known to alert people to danger or fetch help in an emergency. For this reason, a dog is a valuable addition to the family.

5▶ If I **6)** .... **(have)** a dog, I **7)** .... **(look after)** it by feeding it the right food at the right time and making sure it **8)** .... **(have)** plenty of exercise. I **9)** .... **(train)** it to be obedient and take it to the vet for regular check-ups. Perhaps one of the most important things dogs need is affection, because, like humans, they need to feel loved.

6▶ All in all, the effort needed to take good care of a dog is repaid with companionship, loyalty and love. It is easy to see why so many people agree that a dog really is the perfect pet.

1 What type of article is this (description, opinion, or making suggestions/ recommendations)?

2 Is it written in formal or informal style? Why has this style been used?

3 What information has been included in the introduction?

4 What technique has been used to make the introduction more interesting?

5 In the writer's opinion, what is the perfect pet?

6 What reasons does the writer give in support of this opinion?

7 In which paragraphs does the writer give these reasons?

8 What does the writer say about looking after the pet?

9 Are the main points included in clear topic sentences? Underline the topic sentences.

10 Find and underline all the linking words/phrases in paragraphs 2-5. Then, say which ones are used to:

    A list points

    B explain reasons/results

    C introduce examples

11 Read the article again and suggest alternative linking words.

Introduction
• • • • • • • • • • • •
Paragraph 1

mention the perfect pet and state your opinion

Main Body
• • • • • • • • • • • •
Paragraphs 2- 4

reasons for choice of pet

Paragraph 5

how to take care of pet

Conclusion
• • • • • • • • • • • •
Final Paragraph

restate your opinion/ summarise points

6 **Look at the notes below. Match the viewpoints to the reasons/examples, then use your notes to write a main body paragraph explaining why goldfish would make ideal pets.**

Viewpoint		Reason/Example
1 easy to look after		**A** research has shown that watching fish can reduce stress
2 don't make the house untidy		**B** their food costs very little, and they don't have to be taken to the vet
3 are not expensive to look after		**C** you only need to feed them a pinch of food once a day
4 can help you relax		**D** unlike dogs and cats, they don't make a mess

CHOOSING THE CORRECT WRITING STYLE

When you answer an exam question, remember to study the key words carefully to interpret the writing style required — e.g. *a letter to a friend* would require an **informal** style, whereas *an article for a magazine* would normally require a **semi-formal** style.

- **Informal style** — chatty, very personal, colloquial language (i.e. everyday expressions, idioms, phrasal verbs and short forms)
- **Semi-formal style** — polite, respectful but friendly tone (i.e. less colloquial than informal style, short forms used less frequently, linking words/phrases used to connect ideas)
- **Formal style** — official, business-like, polite but impersonal tone (i.e. advanced vocabulary, frequent use of the passive, formal linking words/phrases, no short forms or colloquial language, complex sentences)

7 **a)** **Read the endings and match them to styles A - C.**

A ☐ informal   **B** ☐ semi-formal   **C** ☐ formal

1 To sum up, the Westfield Centre is a modern and well-equipped building in which a range of small and medium-sized conference facilities are available at competitive prices. Despite the limited parking space, the centre is highly recommended as a venue for company training courses.

2 All in all, a good pen friend should always welcome your letters and write interesting replies. What is more, even if you have never met your pen friend, they should be someone you can always turn to as a true friend.

3 Anyway, that's all my news for the moment. I hope you're okay — write back soon and tell me all about your new place.

b) **Read the extracts again and match them to the types of writing.**

A ☐ letter to a friend   **B** ☐ assessment report   **C** ☐ magazine article

c) **Use the prompts below to write the introduction to extract 2:**
What makes a good pen friend?

- what make/good pen friend?
- everyone/have/different answer/this question
- some qualities/we all look for in/pen friend

8 **Read the rubric, underline the key words, then answer the questions.**

> You recently read the following statement in a local newspaper:
> *"Everybody can do something to help reduce crime in their neighbourhood."*
> Write a **composition**, saying whether or not you agree with the statement and making suggestions about how crime can be prevented.

1 Do you agree or disagree with the statement?

2 What expressions/linking words could you use to make suggestions?

9 **Read the article and replace the words in bold with formal ones from the list below. Then answer the questions.**

more difficult, Parents, serious problem, reduce, children, Needless to say, members of the local community

How many of us can honestly say that we live in a neighbourhood that is not affected by crime? Crime is certainly a **1) bad thing** and I agree that everyone can play a part in helping to reduce it.

One way to prevent crime would be for people to pay more attention to what is going on around them. For example, if **2) neighbours** took more notice of their surroundings and reported anything suspicious to the police, fewer crimes would be committed.

Another solution would be to make it **3) a bit harder** for criminals to commit a crime. For example, we could all make sure that we locked our cars and houses securely. If people were more careful, it wouldn't be so easy for criminals to break in and steal things.

It would also be a good idea to educate children about the dangers of getting involved in crime. **4) Mum and dads** and teachers could help, and the police could give talks in schools so that **5) little kids** would learn about the dangers. **6) I don't need to tell you that** this would **7) cut down on** the number of crimes committed by children.

In my view, we all have a duty to make our neighbourhood a safe place to live in, and the sooner we do it the better.

1 Does the introduction clearly state the topic?

2 Does the writer agree or disagree with the statement? Underline the sentence in the introduction which states this.

3 What technique has the writer used in the introduction?

4 What other techniques can be used in introductions to this sort of writing? Suggest a suitable alternative introduction to this composition.

5 Underline the expressions the writer has used to make suggestions.

6 What would result from each suggestion, according to the writer?

7 Suggest a suitable alternative final paragraph.

Introduction
· · · · · · · · · · · · · · · · · · · ·
Paragraph 1

state the topic, agree or disagree

Main Body
· · · · · · · · · · · · · · · · · · · ·
Paragraphs 2- 4

suggestions and results

Conclusion
· · · · · · · · · · · · · · · · · · · ·
Final Paragraph

summarise your opinion

10 **a) Read the rubric, underline the key words and answer the questions.**

You have been doing a class project on road safety. Your teacher has asked you to write a composition about the following statement:

"Everyone can help to make our roads safer."

You should state whether you agree or disagree with this statement and make suggestions about how road safety can be improved, explaining your reasons clearly. Write your **composition** (120-180 words).

1 What style would be the most appropriate for this composition?

2 Which of the following *must* be included in this composition? Tick (✓):

A reasons/examples to support your suggestions ☐

B descriptions of serious accidents ☐

C suggestions about how to reduce road accidents ☐

D agreement/disagreement with statement ☐

b) Read the rubric again. Do you agree or disagree with the statement? Match the suggestions (1-5) with the reasons/examples (A-E), then select the ones that support your views. Finally, make sentences using suitable linking words/phrases, and making any other necessary changes, as in the example.

1 stricter penalties for drivers who break the law

2 pedestrians and cyclists can help

3 people could use their cars less or share with others going in the same direction

4 advertising campaigns to show drivers that dangerous driving can put people's lives at risk

5 improve roads and signposts

Reasons/Examples

☐ **A** heavy fines would make people think twice before speeding

☐ **B** fewer accidents would be caused; drivers able to see stop signs and speed limits better

☐ **C** fewer cars on the road would mean fewer accidents

☐ **D** people would learn that dangerous driving can kill

☐ **E** people should take more care when crossing roads and cyclists should be more alert

e.g. *To begin with, the government should introduce stricter penalties for drivers who break the law. Heavy fines, for instance, would make people think twice before speeding.*

Introduction . . . . . .

Paragraph 1

state topic, agree/disagree

Main Body . . . .

Paragraph 2

first suggestion and reasons/examples

Paragraph 3*

second suggestion and reasons/examples

Conclusion . . . .

Final Paragraph

restate your opinion

* The number of main body paragraphs depends on the number of suggestions you want to include

11 **Read the rubric in Ex. 10 again. Then, write your composition using the plan above, as well as your answers from Ex. 10 (120-180 words).**

12 Read the rubric, underline the key words and answer the questions.

You have seen the following announcement in your local newspaper.

TELL US WHAT *YOU* THINK

The local council will soon decide whether the town of Blakely will have a new sports centre *or* a new entertainment centre.

We want *your* opinion. Write an article telling us which one should be built. Give reasons for your choice and say what you would like the centre to offer.

£25 prize for the best article received.

Write your **article** for the competition.

1 What type of writing is this?

2 Imagine you have chosen the entertainment centre. What reasons could you give to support your choice? What facilities should be provided?

13 Read the article and answer the questions.

As we are all aware, Blakely has been given a sum of money to be spent on either a new sports centre or a new entertainment centre. I believe that the money should be spent on a new entertainment centre.

The main reason is that Blakely already has a wide range of sports facilities. In addition to the football stadium and athletics track, the town has a modern public swimming pool, an ice rink, tennis courts, several gyms and so on. Do we really need a sports centre as well?

On the other hand, there are very few entertainment facilities in the town. There is only one small cinema, the only existing disco is on the outskirts of town, and the nearest theatre is more than 30 miles away.

The proposed entertainment centre should therefore include a theatre, cinema and disco. Furthermore, an exhibition hall should be provided so that lectures and exhibitions could be held. Facilities such as a coffee shop or restaurant would give people the chance to meet and relax before or after a show.

In conclusion, I strongly believe that a new entertainment centre would increase the choice of entertainment in Blakely, and improve the quality of life in our town.

1 What would be a suitable title for this article?

2 Is it written in formal or informal style? Why has this style been used?

3 Which centre does the writer think should be built? What reasons are presented in support of this choice?

4 What facilities does the writer suggest should be provided?

5 Which tenses are used in the model?

6 Underline the linking words/phrases used in the article, and suggest suitable alternatives which could be used to replace them.

7 Suggest an alternative introduction and conclusion for this article.

Introduction

Paragraph 1

state the topic and your opinion clearly

Main Body

Paragraph 2

first reason for choice and justification

Paragraph 3

second reason for choice and justification

Paragraph 4

suggestions for facilities

Conclusion

Final Paragraph

restate your opinion

14 Read the rubric, underline the key words and answer the questions.

> An international magazine is publishing articles for a series called *Influential People of the Twentieth Century*. You have been invited to write a short article about a person who was an influential figure in your country during the twentieth century. Write your **article** for the magazine (120-180 words).

1 What type of writing is this?

2 Could you write about someone from long ago (e.g. ancient times, medieval times, the 1800s)? Why (not)?

3 Who would you write about? Why?

4 When writing about an influential person, what details could you include in your article (e.g. physical appearance, character, interests, historical importance, in what way influential, etc)?

15 Read the article and answer the questions.

> Of all the important people in the twentieth century, without doubt the one who had the most positive influence was Diana, Princess of Wales.
>
> Diana was an extraordinary woman. Her beauty and elegance attracted attention wherever she went and she was often harassed by the press. Nevertheless, she was not discouraged by them. On the contrary, she led a very active life. She also made a point of spending a lot of time with her two sons and was clearly a caring and loving mother. In addition, much of her life was devoted to organising charity events which not only raised money to help the poor, but also made the public more aware of the problems the less fortunate face every day. Her down-to-earth nature and her compassion set an example for others to follow.
>
> Diana was a great influence on the country for many reasons. First, she helped many people through her work, such as AIDS sufferers. She also helped change the negative attitudes many people had towards such illnesses. Furthermore, by coming into direct contact with those she helped, such as children in orphanages or patients in hospitals, she showed that no matter who or what a person is, they should be kind, considerate and helpful towards everyone they meet.
>
> Diana's influence was so great that, even after her death, the good work she started has been continued by others. She is definitely a person not to be forgotten.

Introduction

Paragraph 1

name of person; comment about his/her influence

Main Body

Paragraph 2

brief description of his/her appearance, lifestyle and character, with justification

Paragraph 3

influence & reasons

Conclusion

Final Paragraph

comments and feelings (general, not personal) about the person

1 Is the article written in formal or informal style? Give examples to justify your answer.

2 What is included in the introduction of the article? Suggest an alternative introduction.

3 What is the main point of paragraph 3? Underline the topic sentence.

4 In what ways was Diana influential, according to the article?

5 What explanations/examples has the writer given to show how Diana was influential?

6 What linking words have been used
  – to list points/give examples?
  – to show contrast?

16 Read the rubric, underline the key words and answer the questions.

> An international magazine has asked its readers to send in articles for a special edition about friends and friendship. You have decided to write an article about what makes an ideal friendship. Write your **article** for the magazine (120-180 words).

1 What type of writing is this?

2 In your opinion, what are the most important qualities a friend should have?

17 Read the article and answer the questions below.

What does the word 'friendship' mean to you? For some people, friends are just people you go out and have fun with. For me, however, the ideal friendship is much more than that.

Firstly, a true friend should be honest and trustworthy. Without these characteristics, you cannot have a good relationship with anyone. What is more, both partners in a friendship should have these qualities. A proper friendship is one based on equality.

Secondly, I believe that it is important to share similar interests with your friend. It would be very difficult to keep a friendship going if the two people had nothing in common.

Thirdly, an ideal friend is one who you can turn to in times of trouble. Friendship is not only about having a good time, but being able to give or ask for support whenever it is needed. Some of the closest friendships have developed under very difficult circumstances.

To conclude, there are many people who we can call a friend, but the qualities friendship is built on — trust, shared interests and supporting one another — are harder to find than you might imagine!

1 Suggest a suitable title for this article.

2 Has it been written in formal, semi-formal or informal style?

3 What are the characteristics of this kind of writing? Give four examples from the text.

4 Does the introduction clearly state the topic?

5 Which techniques has the writer used to start the article? Suggest an alternative introduction for this model.

6 In the writer's opinion, what makes an ideal friendship? Has each point been presented in a separate paragraph with a clear topic sentence? Underline the topic sentences.

7 Underline the words/phrases the writer has used to list points. Suggest alternative words/phrases which could replace these.

8 What reasons has the writer given in each paragraph to support the points presented?

9 How does the writer end the article?

Introduction ....

Paragraph 1

introduce the topic

Main Body ....

Paragraphs 2-4

viewpoints and reasons

Conclusion ....

Final Paragraph

summarise points

---

18 Read the rubric, underline the key words and answer the questions.

> You have had a class discussion about the following statement:
>
> *Only people who know how to make music can really enjoy listening to it.*
>
> Now your teacher has asked you to write a composition giving your views on the statement. Write your **composition** (120-180 words).

1 What type of writing is this?

2 Do you play a musical instrument?

3 Do you enjoy listening to music?

19 Read the article and answer the questions.

1▶ Is it impossible to appreciate music, as some people argue, if you don't play a musical instrument yourself? I strongly believe that the ability to enjoy music does <u>not</u> depend on the ability to make music.

2▶ To begin with, people with no musical talent can nonetheless get pleasure out of listening to talented musicians play. My main reason for saying this is based on personal experience. Although I do not play any musical instrument, I enjoy a great variety of music, from classical to rock, and millions of music fans around the world feel the same way.

3▶ Furthermore, liking music is not something that depends on education, knowledge or ability. Instead, music 'speaks' directly to the emotions. This is clear from the way babies and animals respond when they listen to music, which shows that anyone is capable of enjoying music.

4▶ On the other hand, knowing how to play a musical instrument can help you understand music more clearly and appreciate it in a different way. If you write music yourself, for example, you understand more about the music you listen to than someone who does not.

5▶ To sum up, I feel that anyone can enjoy listening to music, whether or not they know how to make music themselves. It is true that musicians probably get greater pleasure out of listening to music than the rest of us do, but this does not mean that our own enjoyment of music is not 'real'.

1 Does the writer agree or disagree with the topic? Underline the sentence in the introduction which states the writer's opinion.

2 What technique has been used in the introduction? Suggest an alternative introduction using a different technique.

3 Has the writer presented arguments both for and against the statement? What are these arguments, and in which paragraph is each presented?

4 Which sentences state the writer's main arguments? What justification has been given to support each argument?

5 Underline the linking words/expressions used in the composition, then suggest suitable alternatives which could replace them.

6 Suggest an alternative conclusion.

Introduction

Paragraph 1

state the topic and your opinion clearly

Main Body

Paragraph 2

viewpoint 1 and reason

Paragraph 3

viewpoint 2 and reason

Paragraph 4

opposing viewpoint and reason(s)

Conclusion

Final Paragraph

restate your opinion using different words

20 Read the rubric, underline the key words and answer the questions.

A friend has written to ask how to improve his/her English. Write a letter in reply, giving your advice. You should also mention the main difficulties which you think your friend might face. Write your **letter** to your friend (120-180 words).

1 What kind of letter is this (an invitation, a letter of complaint, an application for a job, etc)?

2 What advice would you give to a friend who wants to improve his/her English?

21 Read the letter and answer the questions.

Dear Juan,

1 ► Thanks for your last letter. I think it's great that you want to improve your English, and of course I'd be happy to give you any advice I can. Don't worry – I'm sure you'll find it a lot easier than you expect.

2 ► The best thing you can do is to start a course in English. There are lots of schools which offer lessons, and I'm sure they have qualified teachers who will be able to teach you properly.

3 ► If I were you, I'd also try to make friends with someone who is a native English speaker. If you do this, you'll be able to practise what you learn in class — and as they say, 'practice makes perfect'.

4 ► It would also be a good idea to read English magazines or books, and watch films and TV programmes in English. This gives you a lot of useful practice, and it's fun at the same time! If you like, I could send you books and videos from here.

5 ► Of course you will have a few problems, especially at the beginning. The main difficulty is with phrasal verbs, because there are so many of them, and they have so many different meanings! Don't give up — after all, English isn't a difficult language to learn, and you already know the basics.

6 ► Naturally, from now on I expect you to write to me in English as much as you can. If you follow my advice, I'm sure your English will improve in no time. Good luck!

Regards,
Maya

1 Is this letter written in formal or informal style? Why has this style been used?

2 What are the characteristics of this type of writing? Find examples of each characteristic in the letter.

3 What is the reason for writing this letter?

4 What advice has the writer given in the letter? In which paragraph(s)?

5 What words/expressions has the writer used to give advice? Suggest alternative words/expressions which could replace them.

6 When giving advice, the writer gives reasons to explain in what way this will help. Underline each of the reasons given in the letter.

7 Underline the topic sentence in paragraph 5. What is the main point of the paragraph?

8 Suggest a suitable alternative final paragraph for this letter.

Introduction

Paragraph 1

reason(s) for writing

Main Body

Paragraphs 2-4

advice and reasons

Paragraph 5

problems

Conclusion

Final Paragraph

closing remarks

22 Read the rubric, underline the key words and answer the questions.

> Your cousin is worried that he/she won't pass all his/her exams this year and has written to you asking for advice. Write a letter in reply, giving your cousin advice about how to prepare for exams and explaining the main difficulties students face. (120-180 words)

1 What kind of letter is this?

2 What advice would you give someone who wants to prepare well for their exams? What are the main difficulties they might face?

23 a) Read the notes (1-5) below and match them to the reasons (A-E). Then, use suitable expressions and linking words/phrases to write sentences offering advice, together with reasons, as in the example.

1 make study timetable

3 revise questions in past tests/exams

4 use coloured pens to highlight important points

2 get plenty of sleep

5 don't try to study every book in the library

A		you will be able to practise answering exam questions
B		there is a limit to how much information you can learn
C	1	you'll know how much time you've got in order to prepare for each subject
D		you can't learn properly if you're tired
E		it will be easy to find the key points in your notes, and you'll remember these more easily

e.g. If I were you, I'd make a study time-table. If you do this, you'll know how much time you've got in order to prepare for each subject.

b) Use the prompts below, as well as ideas of your own, to talk about the difficulties someone may face when preparing for exams.

• you start to panic as the date of the exam gets nearer

• it's hard to get started – you keep telling yourself you'll start tomorrow

• you get discouraged because you keep forgetting certain information

• ....
....

• ....
....

e.g. Many people start to panic as the date of the exam gets nearer. Try to stay calm, though, because you won't do your best if you're very nervous.

24 Read the rubric in Ex. 22 again, then write your letter (120-180 words). Use your answers from Ex. 23 to help you. You can use the letter in Ex. 21 as a model.

25 **Read the rubric, underline the key words and answer the questions.**

A travel magazine is organising a short story competition for the best story about an excursion to remember. The story must **begin** with the words: *As soon as Bob arrived in the city, he knew that this would be a wonderful day.* Write your **story** for the competition. (120-180 words)

1 Should your story relate to a trip/journey? Why (not)?

2 What kind of day would be 'wonderful'?

3 Should you write your story in the first or third person? Why?

26 **Read the story and answer the questions.**

1▶ *As soon as Bob arrived in the city, he knew that this would be a wonderful day.* He had won a day out in London and tickets to the theatre to see 'On Broadway'. The morning sun was bright and Bob and his brother were excited as they left the station and saw a shiny black limousine waiting to pick them up. As the chauffeur opened the door for them, Bob smiled to himself and felt very important.

2▶ The first thing they did was to go sightseeing. They visited Tower Bridge, then their driver took them to see Buckingham Palace. Neither Bob nor his brother had been to London before and they were amazed by all the huge, beautiful buildings.

3▶ The next thing they did was to have lunch in a famous, expensive restaurant. While they were being led to their table, Bob marvelled at the luxurious decor. As they walked past one table Bob couldn't help staring at some actors whom he recognised from television. This was something to tell his friends about when he got back home.

4▶ Soon it was time to go to the theatre. When the lights went down, Bob whispered to his brother, "This is fantastic! I can't believe we're here!" The performance was incredible. Bob knew that this was an experience he would always remember.

5▶ By the time they got home, they were both exhausted. "What a fabulous day!" Bob sighed happily to himself before falling asleep. "How lucky I was to win the prize!"

1 Underline any information in the introduction which makes reference to:
• the people involved • time • place • weather • feelings

2 How many paragraphs does the main body consist of? What is the main event in each one?

3 Which is the most commonly used verb tense in the story? Why? What other tenses are used, and why?

4 Which word is used:
- in Para. 2 instead of *'big'*?
- in Para. 3 instead of *'looking'*?
- in Para. 4 instead of *'said'*?

5 Underline the words/expressions used to show time and/or sequence of events. Suggest suitable alternative words/phrases.

6 Which words/expressions have been used to express feelings/reactions?

7 Which descriptive adjectives are used to describe:
• the limousine? • the buildings?
• the restaurant? • the decor?
• the performance?

8 Which technique has been used to end the story? What other techniques can be used? Suggest an alternative ending.

Introduction
. . . .

Paragraph 1

Set the scene
(who - where - when - what)

Main Body
. . . .

Paragraphs 2 - 4

Develop the story
detailed description of events in the order they happened

Conclusion
. . . .

Final Paragraph

end the story; final feelings, comments, etc

27 Read the rubric, underline the key words and answer the questions.

You have been invited to write an article for *Screen* magazine, saying whether you prefer going to the cinema or watching videos at home. Write your **article**, saying which you prefer and giving reasons.

1 What type of writing is this?

2 Which do you prefer — cinema or video? Why?

28 Read the article and answer the questions.

CINEMA or VIDEO? by Marty Stevens

1 There has been a lot of talk in recent years about video being responsible for the death of cinema. Despite the fact that videos certainly have advantages, I much prefer going to the cinema, for a number of reasons.

2 Firstly, an evening at the cinema is an exciting outing. You can arrange to meet friends there and you can go for a meal before or after the film. It's a more entertaining way of spending your time than just sitting in your living room.

3 Secondly, modern cinemas have excellent projectors and sound equipment, so the film is much more gripping as a result. When watching adventures or science-fiction films, for example, you really feel as if you are part of the action. This is difficult to achieve at home, however good your television is.

4 Furthermore, I prefer the cinema because I want to see the latest releases. You sometimes have to wait a year for a film to come out on video. By that time, most of your friends have seen it and you have heard so much about the film that it has no surprises.

5 However, videos also have certain advantages. They are cheap and convenient, and you can watch them in the comfort of your own home whenever you are in the mood. You can also watch the video as often as you want.

6 In conclusion, I believe that, although videos have some advantages, people will always be drawn to the attractions of the big screen.

1 Which does the writer prefer — cinema or video?

2 Write a suitable alternative introduction.

3 In which paragraphs does the writer give his/her viewpoints? How does he/she introduce each one?

4 What are the main viewpoints? What reason(s) does the writer give to support each viewpoint?

5 In which paragraph does the writer present the opposing view? What reasons are given to support this?

6 What tenses have been used in this article?

7 Underline the descriptive adjectives, then suggest suitable alternatives which could be used to replace them.

8 Write a suitable alternative conclusion.

Introduction

Paragraph 1

state the topic and your opinion clearly

Main Body

Paragraphs 2 - 4

viewpoints and reasons

Paragraph 5

opposing viewpoint and reason(s)

Conclusion

Final Paragraph

restate opinion using different words

29 Read the rubric, underline the key words and answer the questions.

You have just seen the following advertisement in an international magazine:

WANTED — CHILD-MINDER

We need someone to help during the school holidays. The job involves looking after two energetic children, aged 8 and 9.

The ideal candidate will be:
- a student aged 16-22
- able to speak English
- free for the whole summer
- able to organise children's activities

Please write to Mrs G Miles at the address below.

Write your **letter of application** to Mrs Miles. (120-180 words)

1 What style should this letter be written in? Why?
2 Can you suggest any phrases suitable for such a letter?
3 What kind of person might respond to this advertisement?

30 Read the letter and answer the questions.

Dear Mrs Miles,

1 I am writing with regard to your advertisement for an English-speaking child-minder which appeared in Sunday's edition of *The World Today*.

2 I am a twenty-one-year-old student from Hungary. I have just completed my second year at Loughborough University, where I am studying child psychology. I speak English fluently, as I have been living in England for three years. Prior to this I studied the language in Hungary for seven years and obtained my Proficiency certificate.

3 I enjoy working with children of all ages, and I regard myself as friendly, patient and very responsible. I have experience in looking after children, as I have had child-minding jobs during the holidays, as well as a holiday job at the Sunshine Summer Camp in America last summer. My duties there included organising various sports and activities, which the children enjoyed very much. I enclose references from two of my previous employers.

4 I would like to spend the summer working in England and I feel that I would be suited to the position. If you would like me to attend an interview, I would be glad to do so at any time.

Yours sincerely,

Zoya Rozsa

Zoya Rozsa

1 What is the reason for writing?
2 Suggest a suitable alternative introduction.
3 What personal details (e.g. age) are included in paragraph 2?
4 Underline the personal qualities the writer mentions. What other personal qualities might help to make someone suitable for this job?
5 Why does the writer mention her summer job last year?
6 Suggest a suitable alternative final paragraph for this letter.

Introduction

Paragraph 1

reason for writing

Main Body

Paragraph 2

personal details

Paragraph 3

relevant qualities/ experience

Conclusion

Final Paragraph

closing remarks

---

31 **Read the rubric, underline the key words and answer the questions.**

You have decided to have private lessons to improve your English and you have just seen the following advertisement in your school/college magazine. Read the advertisement and the notes you have made. Now, write a **letter** to Mrs Daniels, giving her the information she needs and requesting the information in your notes.

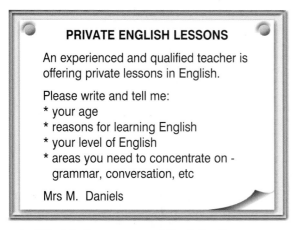

PRIVATE ENGLISH LESSONS

An experienced and qualified teacher is offering private lessons in English.

Please write and tell me:
* your age
* reasons for learning English
* your level of English
* areas you need to concentrate on -
  grammar, conversation, etc

Mrs M. Daniels

Questions for Mrs Daniels

How much?

Where and when?

Many students or just one?

Do I need to buy books, etc?

1 What is the purpose of the letter?

2 What style should it be written in? Why?

3 What information from the advertisement and the notes should be included in the letter?

32 **Read the model and answer the questions.**

Dear Mrs Daniels,

▶1 I am writing in response to your advertisement offering private English lessons, which appeared in the college magazine. I am very interested in the course and would like some additional information.

▶2 I am a nineteen-year-old student at Aston College. I have recently taken the Cambridge First Certificate exam, so I have a reasonable command of the English language. I enjoy learning languages and feel that I have a particular talent in English.

▶3 However, I feel that I need help in the areas of grammar and conversation in order to improve my accuracy and fluency. Furthermore, I am hoping to start a degree course at Southampton University in England next year, so the main reason I need at least Proficiency level English is to enable me to study and socialise there.

▶4 I would appreciate it if you could send me some more information about the lessons offered, such as where and when they would be held, how much they cost and what the price includes. Could you also tell me if there are any extra materials, such as books, which I would be expected to provide? Finally, I would like to know whether you teach students in groups or on an individual basis.

▶5 I will be glad to supply any further information you might need. I look forward to hearing from you soon.

Yours sincerely,

Erik Sorensen

Erik Sorensen

Introduction

Paragraph 1

reason(s) for writing

Main Body

Paragraphs 2-3

give information

Paragraph 4

request information

Conclusion

Final Paragraph

closing remarks

1 In which paragraph is the purpose of the letter mentioned?

2 What details does the advertisement ask for? In which paragraphs have they been provided in the letter?

3 The advertisement asks about "areas you need to concentrate on – grammar, conversation, etc" and "reasons for learning English". What answers have been given in the letter? What linking words/phrases have been used to express reasons? Circle them and suggest alternatives.

4 What information should you ask for, according to the notes? How does the writer introduce each request? Underline these parts.

5 What closing remarks does the letter include? Suggest suitable alternative closing remarks.

33 Read the rubric, underline the key words and answer the questions.

> You have decided to enter a short story competition. The competition rules say that the story must begin with the following words:
> *I will always remember my first day at ...*
> Write your **story**. (120-180 words)

1 Where could you have a "first day"?

2 Should this story be written in the first or third person? Why?

3 In which part of the story (introduction, main body or conclusion) would you write about: - the events of the story, in the order they happened?
- how the story ended and how you felt?
- the place/time, etc in which the story is set?

34 Read the story and answer the questions which follow.

I will always remember my first day at summer school. When I woke up it was a bright, sunny morning — nothing like the awful English weather I'd heard about so often. I was thrilled to be studying in London and the Smiths, the family I was staying with, were very kind and friendly to me. I quickly got ready, had breakfast, then rushed out, feeling very excited.

When I arrived, the college building was huge and I wasn't sure where my classroom was. There was a sea of strange faces and I felt as if I it was my first day at primary school.

Suddenly, I saw someone I thought looked like a girl from my home town. I was amazed when I heard her call out to me.

"Juanita! What are you doing here?" she said.

"Wow, Maria, it really *is* you!" I replied, explaining that I was a student at the summer school. Imagine our surprise when we realised we were both doing the same course!

The summer school turned out to be as good as I had hoped, and my English improved enormously. Needless to say, Maria and I had a great time while we were there, and made lots of new friends from all over the world. She was the last person I had expected to see, but it certainly made the first day one that I will never forget.

1 Underline the information in the first paragraph which tells the reader:
a) when/where the story takes place
b) what the weather was like
c) what the story is about

2 Suggest a suitable alternative introduction for this story.

3 Which words/phrases show the writer's feelings/reactions? Underline them.

4 Which verb tenses have mainly been used in the story? Why?

5 In what way is the conclusion relevant to the first sentence (i.e. the sentence given in the rubric)?

Introduction
. . . .

Paragraph 1

Set the scene
(who - where - when - what)

Main Body
. . . .

Paragraphs 2 - 4

Develop the story
detailed description of events in the order they happened

Conclusion
. . . .

Final Paragraph

end the story; feelings, comments, etc

35 Read the rubric, underline the key words and answer the questions.

> You have been invited to write a short story for an English-language magazine for young people. The editor's instructions say that the story must begin with the words:
>
> *"Don't do that!" I shouted. He ignored me ...*
>
> Write your **story** for the magazine. (120-180 words)

1 What type of writing is this?

2 Should it be written in the first or third person? Give reasons.

3 What might the other person be doing to make you shout, "Don't do that!"?

36 a) Read the beginnings (A and B) below and say which one you prefer for the first paragraph of the story in Ex. 35. Give reasons.

A *"Don't do that!" I shouted. He ignored me* and began to drink what he obviously thought was a cup of tea. Suddenly he started to grow hair and his face began twisting into a vicious expression. "It isn't tea!" I explained, but it was too late. He was already changing into a monster.

B *"Don't do that!" I shouted. He ignored me,* walking towards me with the valuable vase in one hand. John, who was in my class at school, was always joking. That spring morning we had gone to an archaeological museum on a school trip and, as usual, John had got bored. "But it's only a silly old pot," John laughed. I began to feel extremely nervous.

b) Put the events in the order they happened, then tell the story.

A		A young boy pushed me from behind.
B	1	I took the students to the museum.
C		I bumped into John.
D		The curator asked us to leave the building.
E		John took a vase in his hands.
F		The curator caught the vase.
G		I asked John to put the vase back in its place.

37 Read the rubric in Ex. 35 again and write your story (120-180 words). Use your answers from Exs. 35 and 36 to help you.

38 **Read the rubric, underline the key words and answer the questions.**

You are working abroad as a tour guide. Write a letter to a friend at home, describing the job and saying what you like and what you don't like about it. Write your **letter**. Do not write any addresses. (120-180 words)

1 What is the reason for writing the letter? (e.g. giving advice/apologising/etc)
2 What style should it be written in? Why?
3 What are the characteristics of this style?
4 Describe the typical duties of a tour guide.

39 **Read the letter and answer the questions below.**

Dear Helen,

1▶ How are you? Sorry I haven't written sooner, but I've been really busy with my summer job here in London. Anyway, I thought I'd drop you a line and tell you all about it.

2▶ As you know, I'm working as a tour guide for a company called "Star Travel". My job is to look after the people who come on the tour bus and tell them about the history of the places we visit. The company gave me all the information I needed, but I had to study very hard to learn it. Now I'm an expert on all the main London sights, like St Paul's, the Houses of Parliament and the Tower of London. So if you want to know anything, I'm the person to ask!

3▶ What I like most about the job is meeting people from all over the world. So far I've met people from America, Africa and New Zealand. I've even been out in the evenings with some of the new friends I've made.

4▶ The only thing I don't really like about the job is having to get up at six o'clock every morning, in time to greet people as they arrive. You know how I hate getting up early!

5▶ Anyway, I must close now. I hope your family are well. Write back soon and tell me all your news.

Love,
Mary

1 What is the purpose of the letter? Has this been stated in the first paragraph?
2 Suggest a suitable alternative introduction for this letter.
3 In which paragraph is there a description of her job? What does the job involve?
4 What advantages and disadvantages of the job does Mary mention? In which paragraphs does she mention these?
5 What reasons/explanations does she give concerning the advantages and disadvantages?
6 What closing remarks does Mary make? Suggest a suitable alternative final paragraph.

Introduction

Paragraph 1

reason(s) for writing

Main Body

Paragraph 2

description of the job

Paragraph 3

good thing(s) about job, with reason(s)

Paragraph 4

bad thing(s) about job, with reason(s)

Conclusion

Final Paragraph

closing remarks

40 Read the rubric, underline the key words and answer the questions.

> You work for a tourist organisation in a university town with a large number of foreign students. You have been asked to write a report about eating out in your town. Describe the best places for students to eat and drink in the area, and say why you think these places are suitable for foreign students. Write your **report**. (120-180 words)

1 What style should the report be written in?

2 What kind of places would you write about?

41 Read the report and answer the questions.

To: Sandra Walters, Director, Stonebridge Tourist Organisation
From: Eric Johnson, Deputy Director
Subject: Places for students to eat and drink in the Stonebridge area
Date: 6 May, 20....

PURPOSE
The aim of this report is to provide details of places to eat in the Stonebridge area that are suitable for students visiting from other countries.

FAST FOOD RESTAURANTS
There are a number of fast food restaurants in Stonebridge. The two most popular are O'Donnel's in Mill Street and The Burger Palace in Cornwall Road. At either of these places students can enjoy cheap food in clean surroundings. Another advantage is that they have the opportunity to meet local people of their own age.

RESTAURANTS
Many of the town's restaurants can be found in Kingsbury Square. The most popular of these are Tucker's and The Lobster Pot, which have varied menus. Prices are reasonable — about £5 for a main course. Booking is recommended at weekends. Students will enjoy dining in these restaurants, as they offer authentic local dishes in a cosy, traditional atmosphere.

CAFÉS AND BARS
Most of these are located in the old part of town. Davies' Coffee Shop serves sandwiches and pies at reasonable prices. Another favourite is The King's Arms, which has a friendly atmosphere and serves a limited range of home-cooked meals. Both places are recommended for foreign students who want an enjoyable evening out listening to music or dancing.

CONCLUSION
On the whole, the eating places in Stonebridge offer good value and there is enough variety to suit students' individual needs. A visit to any of the above would be an excellent way to meet local people and experience local entertainment.

1 What is the purpose of the report? Is this purpose clearly stated in the introduction?

2 Suggest a suitable alternative first paragraph for this report.

3 Which of the following points are *not* mentioned in each of the main body paragraphs (paras. 2, 3 and 4)?
- most popular places
- location
- size
- type of food
- prices
- decor
- atmosphere/surroundings
- why suitable for students

4 Suggest a suitable alternative final paragraph for this report.

Introduction

Paragraph 1

state the purpose and content of the report

Main Body

Paragraph 2 - 4

summarise each point under suitable sub-headings

Conclusion

Final Paragraph

general assessment and/or recommendation

42 Read the rubric, underline the key words and answer the questions.

> The following statement was printed in an international magazine:
> *A lot of what is taught in school nowadays is not worth learning.*
> Now your teacher has asked you to write a composition on this subject, with reference to your own learning experiences. Write your **composition**. (120-180 words)

1 What type of writing is this?

2 In what style are opinion essays usually written?

3 What does "with reference to your own learning experiences" mean?

4 Do you agree or disagree with the statement? Why?

43 Read the essay and answer the questions.

Although schoolchildren often complain that school is boring and a waste of time, I think this is an exaggeration. In my view, the majority of the things we are taught in school are useful to us in many ways.

In the first place, school gives you general knowledge which helps you in your everyday life. My own experience has shown me that a knowledge of subjects such as Geography and History, for instance, helps to understand what is happening in the world around us. Without this 'background' knowledge, the information in newspaper reports, TV documentaries and so on would mean very little to me.

Furthermore, some school subjects help you develop an interest in hobbies. In my case, I like to spend my free time surfing the Internet. I would find this much harder to do if I had not taken Computer Studies at school.

On the other hand, there are some subjects taught in school which seem to me to be a waste of time. I particularly dislike Algebra, for example, and I cannot see how memorising formulas and equations will ever be useful to me.

To sum up, I believe that, with one or two exceptions, it is wrong to say that what is taught in schools is not worth learning. On the contrary, it gives us a very good basis for our understanding of the world.

1 In what style is this model written? What are the main characteristics of this style? Find examples of each characteristic in the composition.

2 Does the writer agree or disagree with the statement in the rubric? Which sentence states this clearly?

3 Underline the topic sentence in each of the main body paragraphs.

4 In which paragraphs does the writer express viewpoints disagreeing with the statement in the rubric? In which paragraph does she express the opposing viewpoint?

5 What personal examples are given as reasons to support these viewpoints?

6 Underline the linking words/phrases which have been used to:
a) list points,
b) show contrast,
c) introduce personal opinion or experience?

7 Suggest a suitable alternative final paragraph for this composition.

Introduction

Paragraph 1

state the topic and your opinion clearly

Main Body

Paragraphs 2 - 3

viewpoints and reasons

Paragraph 4

opposing viewpoint and reason

Conclusion

Final Paragraph

restate your opinion using different words

44 **Read the rubric, underline the key words and answer the questions.**

You are the secretary of the students' social events committee at your college. Read the note from Jeff, the committee chairman. Then write to the principal, Mrs Roberts, asking for permission to have a party and telling her about the plans that have been made so far. Write your **letter**. Do not write any addresses. (120-180 words)

Please write to Mrs Roberts and ask her if we can have a party in the college canteen. There were some problems last year, so reassure her that there won't be any complaints!

- 8 - 11:30 pm, Sat 28th July
- ticket holders only (400 maximum)
- Sonic Sounds will do the disco (special price!)
- Sarah Shaw's doing food & drink, Ali Lee's doing the decorations

Thanks,
Jeff

1 What is the main reason for writing the letter? What are the two other reasons for writing?

2 What style should the letter be written in — formal or informal? Why?

3 What sort of "problems" might there have been at last year's party? What could be done to make sure these problems did not occur again?

45 **Read the letter and answer the questions.**

Dear Mrs Roberts,

1 I am writing on behalf of the Students' Social Events Committee to request the use of the college canteen for the summer disco, which we are hoping to hold at the end of the college year.

2 We would like to hold the disco on 28th July, from 8:00 pm to 11:30 pm. Entrance would be to ticket holders only and we plan to sell no more than 400 tickets. The music will be provided by Sonic Sounds, who have agreed to provide their services for the evening at a discount price. Sarah Shaw will be organising the food and drink and Ali Lee is in charge of the decorations.

3 I realise that you may be concerned about our making too much noise or leaving the canteen in a mess, as was the case with the last party held there. Let me assure you that we will take precautions to ensure that no complaints are made this time. The disco will finish at 11:30 pm precisely, and members of the committee will make sure that people leave the building quietly, so that there will be no disturbances after midnight. Six members of the committee have also offered to tidy and clean all the rooms after the party.

4 I am sure that you understand how much the summer disco will mean to the students after their hard work throughout the long year. I hope, therefore, that you will give us your kind permission to use the canteen.

Yours sincerely,

Philip Graham

Philip Graham

1 Is the main purpose of the letter clearly stated in the introduction?

2 In which paragraph does the writer tell the principal about plans for the organisation of the party? Have all the details from Jeff's note been included? Underline this information in the letter.

3 In which paragraph does the writer try to reassure the principal that there won't be any problems? What information does he give to support his assurance that precautions will be taken?

4 Suggest a suitable alternative final paragraph for this letter.

Introduction

Paragraph 1

reason(s) for writing

Main Body

Paragraph 2

information about the organisation of the party

Paragraph 3

reassurance that there will be no complaints

Conclusion

Final Paragraph

closing remarks

46 Read the rubric, underline the key words and answer the questions.

> You work for a large company and you organise staff social events. Read the note from your colleague, Martin. Then, write to the director of the company asking for permission to have a party at the office and giving information about the organisation of the party. Write your **letter** in an appropriate style. (120-180 words)

Could you write to Mr Franklin and ask permission for us to have an office party for Sarah's retirement? Remember there were some complaints from local tenants after the last party, so you will have to persuade him there won't be any problems this time! These are the decisions we have made so far:

Date	— 10th May	Food & drink	— Peter
Place	— office	Music	— tapes/CDs
Time	— 6:00 pm - 11:00 pm	Decorations	— Julie

Thanks,
Martin

1 What is the main reason for writing the letter?
2 What information from the note should be included?

47 Read the rubric in Ex. 46 again and write your letter. You can use the letter in Ex. 45 as a model.

48 Read the rubric, underline the key words and answer the questions.

> You have been asked to write an article for your school magazine, suggesting helpful ways of remembering new vocabulary in English. Write your **article** for the magazine. (120-180 words)

1 What type of writing is this?
2 What helps you to remember new vocabulary?

49 Read the article and answer the questions.

Do you spend hours studying new words in English, only to find that after a few days you have forgotten them? Many students have this problem, but you mustn't give up hope. Here are a few ways to help you remember new vocabulary.

One useful method is to write down each new word or phrase on a separate piece of paper. Then you can stick these pieces of paper around your room — on your walls, on a mirror or anywhere you can see them. In this way, you will see the new words every day and you'll soon learn them.

It's also a good idea to choose ten words a week to learn, then ask a friend to test you on their meanings. By learning ten words a week, you will soon build up your vocabulary.

The best way to learn new words, though, is to use them. When you find a new word or expression, look it up in the dictionary to find out what it means, then make sure you include it in your next composition, or in a letter to a pen friend, or even in conversation. After you have used it a few times, you are sure to remember it.

I hope you find these tips useful. Remember, learning English vocabulary can seem difficult, but if you try hard enough, it certainly isn't impossible.

1 Underline the sentence in the introduction which clearly states the topic of the article.

2 What technique(s) has the writer used to make the introduction interesting? Suggest a suitable alternative introduction.

3 What suggestions does the writer make? What results does the writer expect if the reader follows these suggestions?

4 Which expressions have been used to make suggestions? Underline the words/phrases, then suggest suitable alternative expressions.

5 What language has been used to introduce results? Circle the words/ phrases, then suggest suitable alternatives.

6 Suggest a suitable alternative final paragraph.

Introduction

Paragraph 1

state the topic

Main Body

Paragraphs 2 - 4

suggestions and results

Conclusion

Final Paragraph

general comment

50 Read the rubric, underline the key words and answer the questions.

> You recently went to a jazz festival which you thought was fantastic. You have just seen a local newspaper report about the event, which is incorrect. Read the newspaper report, together with your own comments. Then write to the editor of the newspaper, correcting the errors and explaining why you think the festival should be held again. Write your **letter to the editor**. (120-180 words)

FESTIVAL FLOP

It did!
Cyber were first (as in programme)

Not true!

They played for over an hour!

More than 5,000 there!

The Farley Jazz Festival, held last weekend, was very badly organised. According to the programme, the event was scheduled to begin at midday on Sunday, but a series of delays meant that the first group, *Magic*, did not get on stage until 2:30.

With the single exception of Linda Lacely, who was brilliant, all of the performers were second-rate. The festival's main attraction, *West Wind*, played for only half an hour. It is not surprising that the festival was attended by fewer than 2,000 disappointed people.

Do we really want this festival held again next summer?!

1 What type of writing is this?
2 What is the main reason for writing the letter? What is the second reason for writing?

51 Read the letter and answer the questions.

Dear Sir,

1 I am writing in connection with your review of the Farley Jazz Festival, as I wish to point out a number of errors which were included in the article.

2 First of all, your article stated that the first band, *Magic*, were unable to appear at midday as planned. However, the first band was actually *Cyber* (as announced in the programme), and this group did appear at midday.

3 Secondly, the article described the performers as "second-rate". This is not at all fair, since all the musicians were talented and dedicated professionals.

4 The third error was the remark that *West Wind* played for only half an hour. In fact, the group played for at least an hour, and their fans were delighted with the performance.

5 Finally, your article claimed that "fewer than 2,000" people attended the festival. In reality there were at least 5,000 people there, and none of them seemed "disappointed" with the event.

6 I feel the festival should definitely be held again next year, as it provided entertainment for thousands of people and helped the trade at local shops.

7 I hope you will print a correction of the errors contained in your review of the festival, and try to report events with more accuracy in future.

Yours faithfully,
A L Miller
A L Miller

1 What style is the letter written in — formal or informal? Why has this style been used?
2 Suggest a suitable alternative first paragraph for this letter.
3 Underline the information from the newspaper report which has been included in the letter.
4 What useful language has been used to list points? Circle these words/phrases, then suggest suitable alternative expressions.
5 What is the main topic of paragraph 6? What reasons does the writer give to support his/her opinion?
6 Suggest a suitable alternative final paragraph for the letter.

Introduction

Paragraph 1
reason for writing

Main Body

Paragraphs 2 - 5
errors and explanations

Paragraph 6
explanation why festival should be held next year

Conclusion

Final Paragraph
suggested action to be taken/closing remarks

52 Read the rubric, underline the key words and answer the questions.

> A magazine for teenagers is organising a story-writing competition and you have decided to enter. The competition rules state that your short story must begin with the following words:
>
> *I had dreamed of this moment for years, and now I wanted to show that I deserved the chance.*
>
> Write your **story** for the magazine (120-180 words).

1 Is this a first-person narrative or a third-person narrative? Why?

2 How should the story begin? Why?

3 What kind of 'moment' might you dream about for years?

53 Read the model and answer the questions which follow.

I had dreamed of this moment for years, and now I wanted to show that I deserved the chance. I could hardly believe it — I was playing for the school football team at last! As I ran out onto the pitch, the sun was shining brightly and the crowd were cheering loudly.

The whistle blew, and the game began. At first I felt very nervous, but I soon began to relax, and I knew I was playing really well. Both teams were trying hard, but no one could get near the goal. Then, just before half time, Jordan headed the ball to me, I passed it to Wesley, and he scored! The crowd went wild, and I was proud that my pass had helped to put us in the lead.

I was still feeling pleased with myself at the start of the second half. A minute or two later, though, I was running towards the ball when I slipped and fell. It was very embarrassing — but worse than that, after I tried to stand up, I realised I had twisted my ankle and I couldn't walk. As the trainer helped me off the pitch, I felt like crying.

It took me a few days to see the funny side of the story. Now I look back and laugh. It's true what they say — pride comes before a fall!

1 Underline the information in the first paragraph which tells the reader:
   a) where the story takes place
   b) what the weather was like
   c) what the story is about

2 Underline the time words/expressions the writer has used.

3 Circle the phrases which describe feelings/reactions.

4 List the main events in the story.

5 What writing technique has been used in the final paragraph?

6 If the writer hadn't hurt his ankle, what might have happened in the second half of the match? Imagine a different plot line, then write suitable alternative paragraphs for paragraph 3 and the final paragraph.

Introduction

Paragraph 1

Set the scene
(who - where - when - what)

Main Body

Paragraphs 2 - 3

Develop the story
detailed description of events in the order they happened

Conclusion

Final Paragraph

end the story; final feelings, comments, etc

54 **Read the rubric, underline the key words and answer the questions.**

You have had a class discussion about inventions. Now your teacher has asked you to write a composition about what you think was the *best* invention in the last 200 years, and what you think was the *worst* invention during the same time. Write your **composition**, giving reasons for each choice (120-180 words).

1 What type of writing is this?

2 What do you think were the best and worst things invented in the last 200 years?

55 **Now read the composition and answer the questions below.**

Looking back to what life was like two hundred years ago, it is easy to see that the inventions made during this time have resulted in incredible progress. In my opinion, the best of these inventions was the computer, while I believe that the worst was the motor car.

The main reason for choosing the computer is that it allows us to do so many things that we could not do before. In offices, schools and homes around the world, the computer has become such an important piece of equipment that most of us could not imagine life without it. Furthermore, it seems to me that computers will continue to bring us new benefits for hundreds of years to come.

In contrast, the invention of the motor car has brought us more problems than benefits. It is certainly true that the motor car has made travel much easier. However, this same invention also causes terrible air pollution which may put the future of our planet in danger. With the additional problems of traffic jams and road accidents, the motor car has actually made our lives worse, not better.

To sum up, there have been many inventions over the last two hundred years. Some of them, like the computer, have brought us huge benefits. On the other hand, however, inventions such as the motor car have caused a lot of problems which did not exist before.

1 Suggest a suitable title for this composition.

2 What style is the composition written in — formal or informal? Why has this style been used?

3 What does the writer choose as the best invention? What reasons are presented to support this choice?

4 What does the writer choose as the worst invention? What reasons are presented to support this choice?

5 Underline the linking words/ phrases used in this composition.

6 Suggest a suitable alternative introduction for this composition.

Introduction

Paragraph 1

clearly state the topic and your opinion

Main Body

Paragraph

reasons for best invention and justifications/ explanations

Paragraph 3

reasons for worst invention and justifications/explanations

Conclusion

Final Paragraph

restate your opinion

56 Read the rubric, underline the key words and answer the questions.

You saw this announcement in an international magazine for teenagers, and you have decided to write an article.

"My most treasured possession ..."

Write an article with this title, about something of yours that you particularly value. It could be any object, big or small!

You should briefly describe the object, and explain why it is so important to you.

Write your **article** for the magazine (120-180 words).

1 What is meant by the phrase 'treasured possession'? Does the item have to be valuable?

2 What is your most treasured possession, and why do you value it?

57 Read the article and answer the questions.

My Most Treasured Possession ...

by Rebecca Black

Everyone has a certain possession that they would not part with for anything. It may be an object that is worth a lot of money, or it may have sentimental value only. My own most treasured possession is my personal stereo.

This wonderful piece of technology is made of shiny black plastic and is small enough to fit in my coat pocket. It comes equipped with little headphones which are light and comfortable to wear.

One reason I like my personal stereo so much is because it enables me to sit in my room and listen to music while I am doing my homework for college, or when I'm simply relaxing. The sound doesn't disturb my family — in fact, they don't even know when I've got it on!

Another advantage that my personal stereo has is that I can take it everywhere with me. It is my constant companion: on the bus, when out for walks or shopping, and even on the way to and from college. As long as I have music to listen to, I never feel bored or lonely.

My personal stereo is the perfect possession. It provides entertainment, relaxation and companionship, and I would certainly feel lost without it.

1 What style is this article written in — formal or semi-formal? Why has this style been used?

2 Suggest a suitable alternative introduction.

3 Which paragraph includes a description of the object?

4 What reasons and explanations does the writer give for her choice of object? Write an alternative reason and explanation.

5 Suggest a suitable alternative final paragraph.

Introduction

Paragraph 1

clearly state the topic and your choice

Main Body

Paragraph 2

brief description of object

Paragraph 3

first reason for choice and explanation

Paragraph 4

second reason for choice and explanation

Conclusion

Final Paragraph

restate your choice and reasons

58 Read the rubric, underline the key words and answer the questions.

> The editor of an international magazine for young people has invited you to write a short article in answer to the following question:
>
> *If you were asked to choose an everyday object that has changed our lives, which object would you choose, and why?*
>
> Write your **article** for the magazine (120-180 words).

1 What type of writing is this?

2 What everyday objects can you think of that have changed our lives?

3 What object would you choose, and why?

59 Look at the pictures (1-4), name the items, then match them to the notes (A-D). Finally, make sentences using appropriate linking words/phrases.

A
- useful for both computer/music systems — can store information easily
- long-lasting, high quality — production improving all the time

B
- make calls from anywhere — vital to busy people
- especially useful in emergency — e.g. in car, travelling alone

C
- essential tool for business — you can access data quickly
- contact with World-Wide Web — find out about almost anything

D
- learn about the world around you — get latest news, see places you can't visit
- great entertainment — watch whatever/whenever you like, in the comfort of your own home

e.g. *The main reason I would choose the CD is that, since you can store information so easily on a CD, it is useful for both computer and music systems. In addition, ...*

60 Read the rubric in Ex. 58 again and write your article (120-180 words). You may choose one of your answers from Ex. 59 to help you. You can use the article from Ex. 57 as a model.

61 Read the rubric, underline the key words and answer the questions.

> The editor of your college magazine has invited you to write an article suggesting simple ways for students to keep fit and stay healthy. Write your **article** for the magazine (120-180 words).

1 What type of composition is this?

2 What helps you to keep fit and healthy?

62 Read the article and answer the questions.

Common-Sense Fitness *by Susan Murphy*

1 Do you find that most magazine articles about health and fitness suggest 'solutions' that are much too expensive or difficult for you? Well, don't worry — there are a number of easy ways to keep fit and stay healthy.

2 The first step is obvious: if you are a smoker, you should stop. Smoking is a leading cause of cancer, heart disease and a lot of other health problems. It is also bad for non-smokers who have to breathe in other people's smoke. The result of giving up smoking would be a healthier lifestyle, for you and everyone around you.

3 It is also a good idea to get some exercise. You don't need to join a gym to do this. Instead, walk quickly around your neighbourhood for thirty minutes, three or four times a week. If you do this, you will find you have much more energy.

4 Finally, you should make sure you eat healthily, especially if you are overweight. If you cut down on fats and eat more fruit and vegetables, you will lose weight naturally. As a result, you will be fitter, feel better and live longer.

5 So, what can we do to lead a longer and healthier life? The answer is simple. Stop smoking, get some exercise and improve your diet. In my view, these three easy steps are the keys to good health.

1 Underline the phrase/sentence in the introduction which states the topic of the article.

2 What style is the article written in — formal or semi-formal? Why has this style been used?

3 What suggestions does the writer make? In which paragraphs?

4 Underline the phrases used to make suggestions, then suggest suitable alternative phrases.

5 What result does the writer expect if the reader follows each of her suggestions?

6 Circle the phrases used to introduce these results, then suggest suitable alternative phrases.

7 What writing technique has been used in the conclusion? What other techniques can be used?

8 Suggest a suitable alternative final paragraph.

Introduction

Paragraph 1

state the topic

Main Body

Paragraphs 2 - 4

suggestions and results

Conclusion

Final Paragraph

general comment/state your opinion

63 Read the rubric, underline the key words and answer the questions.

You have just seen this advertisement in a local paper.

Film Extras Wanted

We require people of all ages to appear as extras in our next film. Filming will take place in July. You must understand English and be available for at least a week.

To apply, give a full description of yourself, tell us exactly when you would be available, and explain why you would like the job.

Write your **letter of application** (120-180 words).

1 What style should this letter be written in? Why?

2 What is a 'film extra'?

3 How would you describe yourself?

4 Would you like to be in a film? Why/Why not?

64 Read the letter and answer the questions.

Dear Sir/Madam,

I am writing to apply for the position of film extra which was advertised in the Sunday edition of the *Tribune*.

I am a 24-year-old student living in Paris, where I am in my second year of drama school. Before this, I attended a community college in New York, where I studied English and Drama for one year. Although I have not yet had any paid acting experience, I have starred in two college productions.

As regards my appearance, I have long, wavy red hair, a fair complexion and green eyes. I am 1.65 m tall and of average build.

I am particularly interested in this position because I believe the experience would be extremely useful for my studies and my future ambitions.

Since the drama school is closed for the whole of July, I will be available to work at any time.

I may be contacted at the above address, or by telephone on 473-96258. I look forward to hearing from you.

Yours faithfully,

Val Fimbres

Val Fimbres

1 What are the characteristics of this style of writing? Find examples in the letter of each characteristic.

2 What is the reason for writing the letter? Has the writer stated this clearly in the first paragraph?

3 Suggest a suitable alternative first paragraph.

4 Why does the writer want this job? In which paragraph does she state this?

5 Suggest a suitable alternative final paragraph.

Introduction
· · · · · · · · · · · · · · · ·
Paragraph 1

reason for writing

Main Body
· · · · · · · · · · · · · · · ·

Paragraph 2

age, current situation/ relevant studies

Paragraph 3

description of appearance

Paragraph 4

reason(s) for applying/ why you would like job

Paragraph 5

availability

Conclusion
· · · · · · · · · · · · · · · ·
Final Paragraph

closing remarks

---

65 Read the rubric, underline the key words and answer the questions.

You saw this announcement in an international music magazine, and have decided to enter the competition.

> Do you prefer live music or recorded music?
> Write and tell us — and win fabulous prizes in our competition!
> Simply write an article giving your opinion.
> The best article will be published in the magazine and the winner will receive £1000 worth of CDs and concert tickets.

Write your **article** for the magazine (120-180 words).

1 What type of writing is this?

2 Do you enjoy listening to recorded music? Have you ever been to a live concert? Which do you prefer and why?

66 Read the article and answer the questions.

Do you prefer live music or recorded music?

by Tim Jones

Many people say that going to a concert and seeing your favourite group play is a thrilling experience, and one which cannot be compared to listening to recorded music. I disagree with this point of view, for several reasons.

To begin with, there is no doubt that recorded music is more convenient. What could be better than buying a compact disc or cassette and listening to it whenever you want, in the peace and comfort of your own home? Portable players also mean that you can carry the music around with you.

Furthermore, in my opinion the introduction of the compact disc has meant that the quality of recorded music has improved a great deal. When you listen to a CD, you can hear the words and music more clearly than you could at a concert. What is more, you can adjust the volume and so on to suit yourself.

On the other hand, many people argue that the special atmosphere at a live concert makes it more enjoyable. The excitement of the crowd adds to your own excitement, they say, while recorded music can never give you such a feeling.

To sum up, I firmly believe that, although live concerts are often spectacular, you can appreciate a group's music better when it is recorded.

1 What does the writer prefer — live music or recorded music?

2 Underline the main points which the writer gives in support of his opinion. What reason(s) does he present to justify each point?

3 Underline the opposing viewpoint which the writer gives. What reason(s) does he present to justify this point?

4 Circle the linking words/phrases which the writer has used to introduce viewpoints, then suggest suitable alternatives.

5 Suggest a suitable alternative final paragraph.

Introduction
· · · · · · · · · · · · · · · ·
Paragraph 1

state topic and your opinion clearly

Main Body
· · · · · · · · · · · · · · · ·
Paragraphs 2 - 3

viewpoints and reasons

Paragraph 4

opposing viewpoint and reason

Conclusion
· · · · · · · · · · · · · · · ·
Final Paragraph

restate your opinion using different words.

67 Read the rubric, underline the key words and answer the questions.

> You are on the committee of a film club, and have been asked to write a report for the club chairman, suggesting two films to be shown as part of the club's programme. You should briefly describe each film and explain why you think the club members would enjoy these films. Write your **report** (120-180 words).

1 What type of writing is this?
2 What style should it be written in?
3 Which two films would you recommend, and why?

68 Read the model and answer the questions.

To: David Wilson, Chairman, Silver Screens Film Club
From: Jennifer Carlisle, Committee member
Subject: Film recommendations
Date: 4th February, 20....

AIM
The purpose of this report is to recommend two films to be included in the film club's programme for the summer season.

FIRST RECOMMENDATION
The English film *Sleuth* would be a good choice for the June screening. Michael Caine and Sir Laurence Olivier star in this mystery classic. The exceptional thing about this film is that, using make-up, costumes and different accents, these two actors play all the roles in the film.

SECOND RECOMMENDATION
Little Big Man is the second recommendation. This is a black comedy dealing with some serious themes in American history. Dustin Hoffman heads an excellent cast of veteran performers in this epic.

REASONS FOR RECOMMENDATIONS
Both films would offer club members a lot to think about, as well as being amusing and entertaining. This would be a nice contrast to last year's films, which were rather serious. Furthermore, the quality of acting and direction in both films is excellent, which is sure to please our members.

CONCLUSION
For the reasons above, I recommend *Sleuth* and *Little Big Man* as choices for the summer programme. I believe these films would entertain our members and increase attendance at the screenings.

1 Is the purpose of the report clearly stated in the introduction? Suggest a suitable alternative first paragraph for this report.
2 What reasons does the writer give to explain why club members would enjoy the films recommended?
3 Write suitable main body paragraphs about two films of your own choice.

Introduction
· · · · · · · · · · · · · · · ·
Paragraph 1

purpose and content of report

Main Body
· · · · · · · · · · · · · · · ·
Paragraphs 2 - 3

recommendations

Paragraph 4

reason(s) for choices and explanations(s)

Conclusion
· · · · · · · · · · · · · · · ·
Final Paragraph

general comment and final recommendation(s)

69 Read the rubric, underline the key words and answer the questions.

> You belong to a book club and have been asked to write a report for the club magazine, recommending two books to club members. Describe each book briefly and explain why members would enjoy reading them. Write your **report**. (120-180 words)

1 What style should your report be written in?
2 Which books will you recommend, and why?
3 In which paragraph(s) will you:
   - state the purpose of the report?
   - describe each book?
   - suggest reasons why club members would enjoy reading the books?

70 Read the rubric in Ex. 69 again and write your article (120-180 words). Use your answers from Ex. 69 and the plan and model from Ex. 68 to help you.

Appendix I: Linking Words / Phrases

To state personal opinion:	*In my opinion, / In my view, / To my mind, / (Personally) I believe that / I feel (very) strongly that / It seems to me that / I think that* people should be encouraged *to use public transport in the city.*
To list advantages and disadvantages:	*One advantage of / Another advantage of / One other advantage of / The main advantage of / The greatest advantage of / The first advantage of* having your own business is that you do not have to take orders. *One disadvantage of / Another disadvantage of / One other disadvantage of / The main disadvantage of / The greatest disadvantage of / The first disadvantage of* having your own business is that you have to work long hours.
To list points:	*First(ly), / First of all, / In the first place, / To start with, / To begin with, / Secondly, / Thirdly, / Finally,* everyone knows that smoking is extremely bad for one's health.
To show sequence:	*BEGINNING: First, / To start with, / To begin with, / First of all,* get everyone out of the building. *CONTINUING: Secondly, / After this/that, / Then, / Next,* call the fire brigade. *CONCLUDING: Finally, / Lastly, / Last but not least* keep a safe distance from the fire.
To add more points on the same topic:	*What is more, / Furthermore, / Moreover, / Apart from this/that, / In additon (to this), / Besides (this),* dogs are very useful in police work. Dogs are *also* very useful in police work. Dogs are very useful in police work *too*. *Not only* do dogs help the blind, *but* they are very useful in police work *as well*.
To show cause:	*The BBC decided not to show the programme **because / due to the fact that / since / as** it would upset too many people.* *The programme would upset too many people; **for this reason / therefore** the BBC decided not to show it.*
To show effect / result / consequences:	*She won a scholarship **therefore, / so / consequently, / as a consequence, / as a result, / for this reason,** she was able to continue her studies.*
To show purpose:	*He decided to learn Russian **so that** he could read Tolstoy.* *He decided to learn Russian **so as to / in order to** read Tolstoy.*

To give examples:	*For instance,* / *For example,* *by running, swimming or jogging three times a week you feel younger and live longer.* *By taking regular exercise* **such as** / **like** *running, swimming or jogging you feel younger and live longer.* *If you want to feel younger and live longer, you should take regular exercise,* **particularly,** / **in particular,** / **especially,** *running, swimming or jogging.*
To show contrast:	*Seatbelts are known to save lives,* **yet** / **however,** / **nevertheless,** / **but** / **nonetheless,** *many people refuse to wear them.* **Although** / **Even though** / **In spite of the fact that** / **Despite the fact that** *seatbelts are known to save lives, many people refuse to wear them.*
To show time:	*Turn the dial* **when** / **whenever** / **before** / **as soon as** / *the buzzer sounds.* *I haven't been back home* **since** *1982.* *We met* **as** *I was crossing the street.* *I saw him* **while** *I was crossing the street.* *We never see each other* **now that** *they've moved to another neighbourhood.*
Relatives:	*That's the woman* **who** *lives next door to me.* *He's the man* **whose** *car was stolen yesterday.* *That's the cat* **which** *scratched me.* *London is the city* **where** *I was born.*
To introduce a conclusion:	**Finally,** / **Lastly,** / **All in all,** / **Taking everything into account,** / **On the whole,** / **All things considered,** / **In conclusion,** / **To sum up,** *no one is likely to find a cure for the common cold in the near future.*

Appendix IIa: Opening and Closing Remarks for Letters

LETTERS:	INFORMAL	SEMI-FORMAL	FORMAL
Giving news			
Opening Remarks:	(You'll never) guess what ...	I'm writing to tell you about ...	I am writing to inform you of ...
Closing Remarks:	That's all my news for now ...	Write and tell me your news.	I would appreciate your thoughts on this matter.
Making an invitation			
Opening Remarks:	I'm writing to invite you to ...	We would be very pleased if you could come ...	We would be honoured if you could attend ...
Closing Remarks:	Hope you can make it – it'll be great fun!	Please let us know if you can come.	We would be grateful if you could notify us regarding whether ...
Accepting an invitation			
Opening Remarks:	Thanks a lot for the invitation. I'd love to come ...	Thank you for your kind invitation; we would love to join you ...	Thank you for your kind invitation. We would be delighted to attend ...
Closing Remarks:	See you then!	We look forward to seeing you.	Thank you once more for your kind invitation.
Refusing an invitation			
Opening Remarks:	Thanks a lot for the invitation but I won't be able to make it ...	Thank you for your kind invitation. However, we will not be able to come ...	Thank you for your kind invitation. Unfortunately, we will be unable to attend ...
Closing Remarks:	Sorry again. Maybe next time!	Perhaps we can get together soon.	I hope that in the future we might have the opportunity to meet.
Asking for advice			
Opening Remarks:	I've got a problem, and I think you can help.	I'd really like your advice about/ on ...	I am writing to request some advice concerning ...
Closing Remarks:	Write back soon and tell me what you think.	I really hope you can help me.	I would greatly appreciate your assistance in this matter.
Giving advice			
Opening Remarks:	I'm sorry to hear ... and I think I can help.	I'm very sorry to hear that you're having problems with ...	I am writing with regard to your letter requesting advice concerning ...
Closing Remarks:	Let me know what happens.	I hope everything turns out well.	I hope to have been of assistance to you.
Asking for information			
Opening Remarks:	I'm thinking of ... and I wondered if you could help me out.	I'm considering ... and I'd like it if you could give me some information.	I would greatly appreciate it if you could provide me with some information on ...
Closing Remarks:	Hope you can help!	I would appreciate any help you can give me ...	Thank you in advance for your kind cooperation ...

Appendix IIa: Opening and Closing Remarks for Letters

LETTERS:	INFORMAL	SEMI-FORMAL	FORMAL
Giving information			
Opening Remarks:	I've looked into ...	I'm writing in reply to your letter asking for information on ...	I am writing in response to your letter requesting information on ...
Closing Remarks:	Hope this was what you wanted ...	I hope you find this useful...	Do not hesitate to contact me should you require further assistance.
Thanking sb			
Opening Remarks:	Thanks a lot for ...	Thank you very much for ...	I am writing to express my gratitude for ...
Closing Remarks:	Thanks again!	It was very good of you to ...	I am extremely grateful for ...
Apologising			
Opening Remarks:	I'm really sorry about ...	I am writing to apologise for ...	I am writing to offer my sincere apologies regarding ...
Closing Remarks:	Please say you'll forgive me ...	Please accept my apology ...	Once again, please accept our sincerest apologies ...
Congratulating sb			
Opening Remarks:	I'm just writing to say well done ...	I was really happy/pleased to hear that ...	May I congratulate you on ...
Closing Remarks:	Well done!	You really deserve (your) success.	Once again, congratulations.
of Application			
Opening Remarks:	——	——	I am writing to apply for the position ...
Closing Remarks:	——	——	I look forward to hearing from you ...
of Complaint			
Opening Remarks:	——	——	I am writing to draw your attention to ...
Closing Remarks:	——	——	I hope that this matter can be resolved ...
Making Requests			
Opening Remarks:	Could you do something for me?	I wondered if you could possibly do me a favour.	I would be most grateful if you could ...
Closing Remarks:	I hope you can help me out.	I hope it isn't too much trouble.	Thank you in advance for your assistance in this matter.

Appendix IIb: Useful Vocabulary for Letters

LETTERS:	INFORMAL	SEMI-FORMAL	FORMAL
Making an invitation	Let me tell you when & where ... By the way, it's a fancy dress party/formal ceremony ... You can stay over if you like ... There'll be plenty of food/drink ... You won't need to bring anything ...	These are the details of ... It will be a fancy dress party/ formal occassion ... If you need somewhere to stay ... Refreshments will be provided ... It won't be necessary to ...	The party/wedding/ceremony will be held on ... at ... Be advised that the party/ occassion is ... Accommodation can be provided by arrangement ... The catering arrangements have been made ... You will not be required to ...
Accepting an invitation	What a great way to celebrate ... By the way, if you need help with ... Can I bring my friend, Brian?	It's a wonderful way to celebrate ... If you would like any help ... Could I invite a friend to come too?	I'm sure it will be a wonderful occasion. Should you require assistance ... Would it be possible for ... to accompany me?
Refusing an invitation	I can't make it because ... I've got plans for that weekend ...	I won't be able to come because ... I have already arranged to ...	I am unable to attend due to ... I am otherwise engaged ...
Asking for information	Do you know anything about ... I also need to know about ... I want to find out about ... as well. Can you also let me know if ... I would be glad to ...	Do you have information about ... I would also like to know ... In addition, could you tell me ... Please could you also ... I would be grateful for ...	What information do you hold on ... Could you also provide details of ... Furthermore, it would be useful to have information concerning ... Please would you include ... ... would be appreciated ...
Giving information	I have sent you a ... To answer your question about ... Did you know that ...? This information should help you ...	This letter includes a ... In response to your enquiry about ... Were you aware of ...? This information should be useful to you ...	Please find enclosed a ... Regarding your request for ... May I bring to your attention ... The following information may be of use to you ...
Apologising	I'm really sorry for/about ... It wouldn't have happened if ... I admit that it was my fault ... I didn't mean to ...	I apologise for ... It happened because of ... I am to blame for ... It was not intentional ...	Please accept my apologies for ... The situation arose due to ... The fault is entirely mine ... It was not my intention to ...
Making requests	I really need ... Can I ask you to ...	I'd like ... Could I ask you to ...	I wish to request ... Would it be possible for you to ...
Giving advice	Why don't you ...	If I were you, I'd ...	I would suggest that ...

Appendix III: Rules for Punctuation

CAPITAL LETTERS

A capital letter is used:
- to begin a sentence.
  e.g. *There's a great film playing at the cinema.*
- for days of the week, months and public holidays.
  e.g. *This year, Christmas Day falls on the last Sunday of December.*
- for names of people and places.
  e.g. *My best friend's name is Claire and she's from Cardiff, Wales.*
- for people's titles.
  e.g. *Mr and Mrs Graham; Dr Stevens; Professor Brown; etc.*
- for nationalities and languages.
  e.g. *They are French.*
  We love Italian cuisine.
  He's fluent in Portuguese and German.
- for the first word and/or the most important words (e.g. nouns, verbs, adjectives, adverbs) of titles of books, films, plays, TV programmes, etc.
  e.g. *The Sixth Sense*
  Indiana Jones and the Lost Temple
  Alice in Wonderland
  Note: The personal pronoun I is always a capital letter.
  e.g. *George and I are going to the funfair.*

FULL STOP (.)

A full stop is used:
- to end a sentence that is not a question or an exclamation.
- e.g. *I'm having a wonderful time. There's so much to do here.*

ITALICS

Italics are used:
- to show the titles of books, plays, newspapers, films, etc.
  e.g. *The Hunchback of Notre Dame*
  Romeo and Juliet
  The Daily Mail
  Braveheart
- to show names of hotels, restaurants, etc.
  e.g. *The Majestic Hotel*
  Cleo's Grill House

COMMA (,)

A comma is used:
- to separate words in a list.
  e.g. *We need eggs, milk, cheese and butter.*
- to separate phrases or clauses.
  e.g. *He stopped walking, looked down, and realised that he was still wearing his slippers.*
- to separate long sentences linked by *and, but, as, or,* etc.
  e.g. *Susan had a very bad cold, **but** she still went to the party.*
  *Ann brought some delicious egg sandwiches, **and** Tim brought his famous chocolate brownies.*
- to separate a non-identifying relative clause (i.e. a clause giving extra information which is not essential to the meaning of the main clause) from the main clause.
  e.g. *Maria, who is a ballerina, lives in Paris.*
  The local market, where you can buy exotic spices, is located on the High Street.
- after certain linking words/phrases (e.g. in addition to this, for example, however, in conclusion, etc).
  e.g. *In addition to this, Fred is a collector of antique watches.*
- when if-clauses begin sentences.
  e.g. *If we had taken her advice, we wouldn't have got lost.*
  Note: No comma is used, however, when the if-clause follows the main clause.
- before and/or after expressions such as: *he/she said, said Tom/Mary,* etc. when reporting someone's exact words.
  e.g. *Opening the door, he said, "Wake up children, it's time to get ready for your trip."*
  but: *"I am exhausted," said the firefighter.*
- to separate question tags from the rest of the sentence.
  e.g. *Ms Jones is your history teacher, isn't she?*

QUESTION MARK (?)

A question mark is used:
- to end a direct question.
  e.g. *How old are you?*
  Note: A question mark is not used to end an indirect question.
  e.g. *He asked me how old I was.*

EXCLAMATION MARK (!)

An exclamation mark is used:
- to end an exclamatory sentence, i.e. a sentence showing admiration, surprise, joy, anger, etc.
  e.g. *That's great news!*
  What a beautiful baby!

QUOTATION MARK (' ' " ")

A quotation mark is used:

- in direct speech to report the exact words someone said.
  e.g. *'My flight is leaving at 9am,' said Pamela.*
  'Where are you from?' he asked us.
- for quotations (i.e. phrases taken from books, plays, etc), sayings and proverbs.
  e.g. *All in all, I believe that life would be boring without music. As Robert Fripp once said, "music is just a means of creating a magical state."*
  My grandfather used to say that 'an apple a day, keeps the doctor away.'

COLON (:)

A colon is used:

- to introduce a list.
  e.g. *There were four of us on the boat : my mother, my father, my cousin Jane and me.*

SEMICOLON (;)

A semicolon is used:

- instead of a full stop, sometimes to separate main sentences when their meaning is connected.
  Semicolons are not used as frequently as full stops or commas.
  e.g. *Some teenagers find it extremely hard to choose a career; others consider it a fairly easy choice.*

DOTS (...)

- Three dots are used to show that words have been left out from a quotation, proverb, sentence, etc.
  e.g. *As Edward Guthman once said, 'Thirty seconds on the evening news is worth a front page headline ...'*

BRACKETS ( )

Brackets are used:

- to separate extra information from the rest of the sentence.
  e.g. *These days, you can buy popular newspapers (i.e. The New York Times, Le Monde, etc) almost anywhere in the world.*

APOSTROPHE (')

An apostrophe is used:

- in short forms to show that one or more letters or numbers have been left out.
  e.g. *I'm (= I am) writing because I've (= I have) got great news.*
  I left for Canada in the summer of '95. (= 1995)
- before or after the possessive -s to show ownership or the relationship between people.
  e.g. *Tom's bicycle, my sister's son* (singular noun + 's)
  my parents' car (plural noun + ')
  women's shoes (Irregular plural + 's)

Study the examples:

e.g. *Look at that peacock! Aren't **its** feathers beautiful?*
(its = possessive adjective)

but: *It's (= it is) a beautiful day, isn't it?*
Our school is very big. It's got (= it has got) three floors and a huge gymnasium.

- to form the plurals of letters, numbers or abbreviations.
  e.g. *She often writes j's instead of g's.*
  Package holidays became extremely popular in the 1980's.
  UNICEF's efforts to raise money for children living in developing countries have been extremely successful.

HYPHEN (-)

A hyphen is used:

- to form a compound word.
  e.g. *kind-hearted; ten-year-old boy; seventy-nine; tape-recording; well-dressed; water-ski; etc.*

DASH (—)

A dash is used:

- in informal English, the same way as a colon or semicolon.
  e.g. *There are three things I couldn't imagine living without — my best friend, a good book and my dog.*
- to introduce something that you thought of or added later, or something surprising, unexpected, etc.
  e.g. *They're closing down the old library — at least that's what I've heard.*